Unleash The Millennials

Unleash The Millennials
and Save the World

COACH
Millennials in the workplace and survive
the cresting millennium change cycle (MCC)

EMPOWER
Engagement, Productivity, and Loyalty

ACCELERATE
Development, Advancement, Work/Life Balance

INSPIRE
Life Meaning, Purpose, and Calling

MILLENNIALS - NOW IS YOUR "GO" TIME!

Philip Zimmerman

Copyright © 2020 Philip Zimmerman

All rights reserved

ISBN-13:9781690844341

DEDICATION

I dedicate this book to my daughters, Magan and Rachel, and their Millennial peers who will rescue the world from coming calamity in the days ahead. You have been uniquely prepared to address what is occurring in the world—a global pandemic; acceleration of a millennium change cycle (MCC); mass exodus of Boomers from the workplace; reestablishment of truth and knowability in a new philosophic Age; and full emergence of the Connected Age. Be strong and courageous and fear not for you are part of the most educated generation in human history and fully digitally equipped to face the unknown that lies in our collective future.

This book would not have been possible without guidance along the way by mentors and coaches who have molded me to this day. These include my parents, Harry and Evelyn Zimmerman; my first vocational boss, Raul Gonzales; my first intellectual influencer, Jack Hill, Ph.D.; my first mentor and vocational career coach, Richard Adams; my father in the Christian faith, Donald Tabb; and most significantly, my wife, Jennifer, who has stuck with me, supported me, and challenged me to accept and "be" who I was created to be.

And finally, my life, work, and faith are the result of a gracious and loving God who has continued to direct my steps exactly where they are supposed to be along a path chosen by the desires of my heart. I've found this to be true; God rewards those who earnestly seek him.

Unleash The Millennials and Save the World

Table of Contents

	DEDICATION	v
	PREFACE	ix
1.	Going Through A Millennium Change Cycle (MCC)	1
2.	While We Were Sleeping	A Boomer & Xer Story	13
3.	Who Are Boomers?	Oldest Generation in Workforce	21
4.	Where Are Missing Xers?	They were never BORN!	29
5.	Work	Generational Differences are Significant	35
6.	Cultural "Age" Shifts	Philosophic and Business Model	41
7.	Philosophical Collapse	End of Modern Philosophy	47
8.	Economic Shift	End of Industrial Age	55
9.	Technologic Shift	Beginning of Connected Age	61
10.	Pedagogic Shift	Educating Connected Age Workforce	67
11.	Who Are Millennials?	Welcome to Connected Age	75
12.	Coaching	Most Effective Method to Unleash Millennials	87
13.	Engagement	Life Meaning and Drivers for Development	101
14.	Productivity	Life Purpose and Drivers for Advancement	111
15.	Loyalty	Life Calling and Drivers for Work/Life Balance	119
16.	Boomer Paradigm	No Meaning, Purpose, and Calling	133
17.	EPL	Where Fact Meets Fantasy	137
18.	EPL Coaching	Gateway to Creativity and Innovation	145
19.	Unleashing the Millennials	Begin to Save the World	175
20.	Truth and Knowability	Value of Company Values	185
21.	Dawn of Millennial Age	Unleashed Millennials	191
	END NOTES	197

Unleash The Millennials and Save the World

PREFACE

The World Needs Saving

The COVID-19 global pandemic has accelerated the full effects of a millennium change cycle (MCC) that will radically transform all aspects of cultural and business interactions globally. No matter the path back to a theoretical normal life and business in the United States (U.S.), the normal we used to know is gone forever and it is not because of Coronavirus. The aforementioned MCC in all of its fullness would have happened within the next fifteen years had not a virus outbreak and escape from China accelerated its eventuality. Be encouraged, the Millennial generation has been specifically educated and prepared to quickly guide us through rapid cultural and business transformation and safely over the precipice of the MCC.

History records things on earth occur in cycles whether physical or biological; long and short cycles with slight to dramatic affects. Cycles have beginnings, middles, and endings. In early 2020, we were in the late stages of a MCC that began in the 1950's with a likely climax around 2025. This climax is now only a few short years away with dramatic cultural and economic changes possibly not equaled anywhere on earth in over 1000 years. The effects of the MCC so far have been reported in the media as unhinged extremism on both sides of the political spectrum and business sector upheavals due to technological revolutions in national and global

Unleash The Millennials and Save the World

economic activity. Because of the pandemics quickening of the MCC, radical cultural and business transformations will spread throughout the workplace by 2025. Millennials are the only generation in the workplace who are ready to handle the coming changes and through their work Save the World from our current potential to utterly destroy it.

Up until about 2014, plethora of articles, studies, and books describing the Millennial generation propelled a myth that resulted in Millennials becoming the most misunderstood, mischaracterized, and most lampooned generation perhaps in recorded history. While this myth still lingers today, the truth is, Millennials are the most educated and well-prepared generation for workplaces they expected to enter. They do not think they are entitled, broken, or need someone else to fix them. They do feel their education is underappreciated, their skills underutilized, and their workplace contributions undervalued. That is all about to change as the workplace they expected, but did not encounter, is now upon us.

In most simple terms, Millennials in the workplace have been wanting, asking, and waiting for three things for the past ten-years, vocational development, career path advancement, and work/life balance. And for the past ten-years many Boomer and Xer supervisors have simply responded by demanding Millennials take their seats, do their jobs, and stop asking so many questions. This divergent reality between generations in the workplace as recorded in abundant news and journal articles and research data is not normal. The coming MCC in all business sectors will be brought about by what has been influencing this workplace divergence; and again, it is not Coronavirus.

This book was written to encourage, empower, and unleash Millennial talent and younger Xers in the workplace to join a community of like-minded and passionate superheroes engaged in changing social and business cultures and literally save the world from cataclysm. Their immediate areas of influence include establishing common truth and knowability in the workplace and directing business model transformation paths forward as AI enters the workplace and all Boomers and some older Xers leave. Coronavirus did not cause the transformation, merely hastened it.

As the pandemic loosens its grip on social distancing Millennial superheroes will rapidly develop and advance into highest positions of authority in all business sectors. They will quickly establish new

The World Needs Saving

workplaces of authenticity and vulnerability, creativity and innovation, and optimized work/life balance. Metrics and measurements of engagement, productivity, and loyalty (EPL) will all be reinvented. And all this will actuate in the next three to five years as 2025 approaches.

It was not by accident or serendipitous that Millennials are like they are; they have been prepared specifically since the time they were born for such a time as this. The huge, dark, and scary unknown that older generations knew was coming is now here. Millennial superheroes it is time for you to step up, put-on your game face, and overcome what is about to step into the workplace from the "Upside Down." Survival of the U.S. as a culture and economic superpower is fully dependent upon you and your collective success; this is your generations purpose! Lean into it NOW!

This book was also written for Boomers and older Xers to help them recognize the significance of the MCC coming into the workplace and why Millennials are the only ones who can stand against the tide of change and save our culture and the world for our children, grandchildren, and great grandchildren to inherit. It is time older generations in the workplace take a stand and promote, support, and encourage Millennials receiving rapid development thru engagement in institutional knowledge transfer, advancement along career paths thru productivity, and optimal work/life balance thru vocational loyalty. We older generations are too old to effectively engage in the MCC battles at the front lines, but we can support out best and brightest by giving them everything they need to succeed. Unleash The Millennials and Save the World!

I graduated college with a MS & BS in civil engineering at the beginning of the 1980's. My first full-time position was with a new environmental engineering firm stared by a masterful strategic planner, organizer, and leader who delivered superior work products. As we grew from two to sixty-five people in four office locations, he constantly coached me in becoming my best with the intent to one day see me open my own company; which I did six years after he hired me. I spent the next fifteen years in executive leadership of consulting companies actuating very profitable businesses and coaching other people to fulfill their life calling.

In 2000, I decided to pay forward to the next generation and went back to school and earned a Master of Divinity degree. That opened a door to become an educator at an 800+ student pre-K to 12 private Christian college preparatory school. For twelve years I was immersed in everything Millennial teaching 6-8th grade science, junior and senior Bible classes, and developing an Institute of Leadership to train, empower, and send Millennial leaders onto college campuses across the country.

In 2010, I began an organizational leadership Doctor of Ministry program to gain needed knowledge and insight to envision, develop and launch the afore mentioned Institute of Leadership. It was while doing doctoral level background research on Millennials I discovered something was not right generationally in the workplace. The Millennial generation I knew as bright, inquisitive, creative, innovative, and passionate about doing great things in the future were being disparaged for a lack of engagement, productivity, and loyalty in the workplace in technical journals, on-line articles, books, and research based academic studies. It took a deeper dive into the metrics and measures of the research to fully comprehend the issue.

Based upon my research findings my doctoral dissertation project was to develop a workplace implemented coaching program for enhancing Millennial engagement, productivity, and loyalty (EPL) in the workplace. Continued research discoveries of Millennials in the workplace were so alarming it was self-evident the greatest crisis was not in the classroom but in the boardrooms and C-suites of corporations about to experience extreme transformational change. Concurrently with writing my dissertation I entered a coach training program and completed rigorous academic classes and applied method coaching engagements that allowed me to apply for and receive designation as a Professional Certified Coach (PCC) from the International Coach Federation (ICF). Since 2014, I have been helping executives and their executive teams prepare their Millennial talent to lead the effort in addressing dramatic changes rapidly approaching the workplace.

While I do include pertinent parts of my research findings in this book, it is not an academic work. What you encounter reading the book reflects at times personal perceptions and observations of a Boomer generalizing a rapidly transitioning workforce in an equally rapidly transforming workplace within a diverse and increasingly complex melting pot culture.

I've been as generic as possible when dealing with spiritual and supernatural topics that are central to our situation at hand. I fully recognize most corporations and workplaces in general operate within the

The World Needs Saving

framework of a secular society that demands a similar secular workplace environment. In addition, I limit my observations to our Western culture recognizing fully I am leaving out Eastern influences of other parts of our world. Our kids and grandchildren may all be speaking another language one day, but for now our workplace talent and culture are predominantly influenced by Western and not Eastern thinking.

Directed toward the workplace environment, this book presents the reasons why Millennials are perceived to be different, and they are, and why their difference will make all the difference to our future survival. Unleash The Millennials and Save the World is not meant as a trite book title, as you will see herein. Millennials are our best, and really, our only hope of a sustainable Western culture in the future as the MCC reaches its zenith in a few short years. And their place of standing firm and standing against what could be disastrous MCC consequences to our culture is in the workplace.

While the book has a Millennial workplace focus, the principles for moving forward are the same for individuals in and out of the workplace. If you are a Millennial superhero still struggling to get vocational traction or direction, this book will help you get started. If you are the parent of a Millennial who you believe is floundering, you may discover in this book that flounders are a prized fish when allowed to swim in optimal waters. This book may help you get your now adult kids into the proper environment where they will thrive.

One of the serendipitous revelations made while writing this book was the interrelationship of the following three tiers of threes:

Tier 1—Engagement, Productivity, and Loyalty

Tier 2—Development, Advancement, and Work/Life balance

Tier 3—Meaning, Purpose, and Calling

Life meaning is discovered thru engagement and development for "work!" Life purpose is experienced when productivity fosters advancement along a career path. And finally, Life calling is affirmed when achieving work/life balance created by loyalty within a particular vocational field.

Unleash The Millennials and Save the World

All Millennials are needed and must be inspired, empowered, and set loose to intentionally focus on keeping the lid on the proverbial pot when the workplace stew comes to a rapid boil around 2025. I cannot be more confident that if we Unleash The Millennials now in the workplace, they will Save the World for their children and grandchildren to enjoy.

CHAPTER 1

Going Through A Millennium Change Cycle (MCC)

With the Coronavirus accelerating the pinnacle of a millennium change cycle (MCC) already in progress, what do the top drivers for Millennial engagement, productivity, and loyalty (EPL) in the workplace have to do with the end of the world as we know it—Everything! Top drivers for Millennial EPL include the desire for vocational development, opportunities for career path advancement, and work/life balance. These top Millennial workplace EPL drivers have gone unmet for over ten consecutive years and have been pointing to significant cultural shifts which precipitated the MCC and extend beyond normal generational differences. Assimilation, synthesis and surfacing of these shifts in the workplace will soon drastically change everything thought normal today as we Unleash The Millennials and Save the World.

Please bear with me throughout this book as I attempt to concisely explain something precariously complex (i.e. a MCC) that by 2025 will result in extremely good or bad consequences in the United States (U.S.) with little or no middle ground. And the ones who will determine the direction we head are Millennial talent in the workplace. Unleash The Millennials and Save the World as the title of this book reflects the urgency and extent of our uncertain times.

Generational changes in the past often had common cries from older generations that the world as they knew it was coming to an end; and yet the world pushed forward. There are also times in history where MCC's come and the world as people knew it changed as well. We are now in such a MCC; the consequence of which could be catastrophic. This is not written as hyperbole but accurately portrays where we find ourselves in the world.

I'll use the metaphor of a tsunami as the means to help visualize what is coming by 2025. A tsunami is a massive and destructive sea wave initiated when a seismic shift or volcanic eruption occurs on the ocean floor. Unless warnings are given and heeded, peaceful coastal residents in the path of a tsunami get caught up with their communities as they are plowed over by an unstoppable mound of fast-moving water.

A MCC tsunami to soon hit our workplaces was initiated by two massive cultural "Age" shifts occurring over the past fifty years. The early effects of these "Age" shifts in the workplace have delayed Millennials receiving vocational development, career path advancement, and work/life balance. One Age shift was philosophic (i.e. simultaneous end of Modern Philosophy and Age of Western Philosophy and beginning of Postmodern period) and the other Age shift was our business model paradigm (i.e. end of Industrial Age of business and beginning of Connected Age).

The force of this twin-cultural "Age" shift triggered the MCC and will likely, if left unchecked, like a tsunami level to the foundations many long held thoughts in the U.S. about religion, humanity, society, laws, government, education, and freedom. Overnight our thoughts about how to conduct business, fund debt, and determine the value of money can change. The full impact of the MCC tsunami will be felt in the workplace no later than 2025 as the MCC crests and the number of Millennial workers far outnumber other generations in the workplace.

Following an actual tsunami surge is a short lull and then rapid dispersion of water into low lying areas and back into the confines of the ocean beach line. The initial response as the water subsides is to find and rescue survivors of the inundation. Simultaneous with the rescue response are mobilization and the reestablishment of critical societal needs; power, clean-water, food, medical and emergency facilities. This is followed by debris removal, demolition, and finally sanitation (sewer and trash). It is at this point where decisions are made to reestablish former communities and future levels of protection against future inundations. Slowly and steadily businesses begin to re-open and commerce creates opportunities

Going Through A Millennium Change Cycle (MCC)

for continued growth. The full extent of the recovery will not be witnessed for at least another generation or two.

The coming MCC tsunami surge, accelerated by Coronavirus, will not fully recede until a new philosophic Age is established to replace current Postmodernism. What will be happening in the workplace and effecting culture as the surge recedes will be dominated by the philosophic recovery of truth and knowability and continued morphing of the Connected Age business model once transformation is complete. The favorable modulation of the MCC tsunami surge can be highly influenced by empowering Millennial talent thru rapid vocational development, career path advancement, and work/life balance. The "Why and How" to do that is the focus of this book.

Millennials make up fifty percent of the U.S. workforce and will be seventy-five percent of the global workforce by 2025.[1] Ernst & Young and Accenture are reporting that seventy-five percent of their workforces are already Millennial.[2] Yet in 2020, despite their majority and growing numbers in the workplace, the cultural "Age" shifts and resultant MCC have delayed Millennials from receiving development, advancement, and work/life balance; the top drivers of Millennial engagement, productivity, and loyalty.

History shows it takes at least a generation or two or more to resolve a philosophic "Age" shift. The business model "Age" shift will also likely continue to morph for a least another generation or two before finally establishing long lasting foundational elements. By 2040, the Millennials and the generation still in college and below, Gen-Z, will be working in a future totally unrecognizable to the citizens of the Western world today. The coming change is not a routine generational succession but a millennium change.

Let's take a look at two millennium changes that have happened in the past to get an idea of what we may be facing. Did you know we really have no certainty how the Egyptians built the Great Pyramid of Giza (approx. 2560 BCE) and couldn't reproduce it today without great difficulty and expense even with our most advanced technologies and construction methods? The Great Pyramid is only one of many pyramids built in Egypt and in other locations throughout the world. While many theories have been put forth, it is obvious to me and many others what they did is shrouded in mystery. What we do know is that the Great Pyramid has been recognized throughout history as one of the seven wonders of the ancient world. When it was built, its height was approximately 481 feet (think of a 48-story building) and it remained the tallest structure in the world until possibly the Lincoln Cathedral was built in 1311 CE. While it may look disheveled today due to 4500 years of weathering, it was constructed with over two and a half million finely hewn and fitted stone blocks with an average weight of two and a half tons each (most blocks range from two to thirty tons each, with some blocks over fifty tons). It had an outer shell of as many as 144,000 highly polished limestone casing stones weighing fifteen tons each. It is thought that the brilliance of sunlight reflected off the mantle made it visible from the mountains of Israel over 300 miles away.

At its base the Great Pyramid covers a staggering fourteen acres. Inside, there are intricate passages, ramps, rooms, and shafts each of which has been studied thoroughly with many fascinating theories about what purpose they served. It is the most accurately aligned pre-modern structure with true north with only $3/60^{th}$ of a degree of error (note: true north is not magnetic north). It is located at the exact center of the landmass of the earth (note: look this up; pretty amazing factoid).

Here's the issue at hand with the Great Pyramid. It is there in plain sight and has been in plain sight for over 4600 years. Yet, when we casually observe it in our mind's eye we just think, wow that is a really big pile of cut stones. It is not until we realize it is not a pile of cut stones but a masterfully designed, advanced technology, artisan crafted, and perfectly constructed monument crying out to us that something is before our eyes which we cannot explain. A MCC shift happened after the completion of the Great Pyramid such that humans lost the knowledge of the construction methods and technologies used to build this wonder of the world. Its significance for us today is we are living through such a MCC shift with no true understanding of whether in our future we will land on Mars or forget what computers are.

A couple of millennia after the Great Pyramid of Giza was constructed, we find the Mesoamerican Mayans (approx. 2500 BCE-800 CE) were using a celestial calendar system which was the most accurate time keeping system until the cesium (atomic) clock was invented in 1949 (sidebar: Mayan's were also pyramid builders). The Mayans used two independent but synchronized calendar systems that reached the same point every fifty-

Going Through A Millennium Change Cycle (MCC)

two years. They also had a long cycle calendar that repeated about every 7885 years. And then the Mayans disappeared into the woods; no one knows where they went or why. Nor do we know how they ever developed their celestial calendar or if and how they found one developed earlier. Something happened that brought this calendar into existence (we can't deny that) and something happened (i.e. a MCC) that eliminated their society and culture. We are now transitioning through such a time as that. We may not just walk into the woods, but will we still inhabit our major cities?

Will distant future generations look back at this time we are living in and marvel at what the Millennials accomplished with world-saving creativity and innovation during our own MCC? Or will our MCC result in a total loss of technology and culture as we know happened with the Egyptians and Mayans respectively? I say Unleash The Millennials now in the workplace and greatly increase their chance of saving the world as we know it.

The philosophic cultural "Age" shift occurred in the 1950's when Modern Philosophy, the third philosophy of the 2600-year Age of Western Philosophy, ended its influence in the West. We in the West are currently living in a temporary time of philosophical skepticism termed the Postmodern Period (i.e. after Modern). Claims to know "truth" or knowing anything with certainty are met with cynicism. This was a shift from classical philosophic tradition into "anti-philosophy" which is dangerous. In postmodernism no authority above the individual is modulating the flow of ideas; and ideas have consequences. We are in a philosophic morphing space only occupied on two prior occasions in the Age of Western Philosophy over the past 2600 years. The Age of Western Philosophy began with 1100 years of Ancient Philosophy that morphed into 1100 years of Medieval Philosophy that morphed into 400 years of Modern Philosophy. Western culture is at the beginning of only the 3rd such philosophic morph in 2600 years. THIS IS HUGE NEWS!!

While Modern Philosophy and the Age of Western Philosophy are currently dead, the philosophies of the East are still up and running in the cultures in which they predominate. Our focus in this book is the U.S. and we will therefore throughout the book limit our philosophical discussions to our Modern and the Age of Western Philosophy heritage.

Unleash The Millennials and Save the World

The coming MCC philosophic "Age" shift effect in the workplace will directly influence our capitalism-based business environment, economy, and Western culture. Imagine all laws, judicial precedent, and governmental regulations being ignored by business leaders at the highest levels with no consequences. In the absence of accepted and respected philosophical foundational mechanisms of transcendent truth and knowability history shows cultural consequences include chaos, rebellion, anarchy, and enslavement. Millennials in the workplace must grasp and maintain some semblance of our former Western Philosophy principles of transcendent truth and knowability until they or Gen-Z can develop and establish a new philosophic age.

Boomers, more than any other generation in the workplace, can identify what it was like to live in a U.S. social and business culture where Western Philosophy undergirded our thinking; up was up, laws were enforced, mass murders rarely occurred, the public had a knowledge and respect of biblical and moral principles, and privacy was respected. Over the past fifty years all these areas and countless others are unraveling in the general culture and the workplace at an increasing rate. Left unchecked, while we may still be around, life as we now know it in the West could become increasingly difficult in the U.S. and globally in very short order.

The MCC business model "Age" shift was initiated in the mid-1960's and should be completed by 2025. Our centuries old Industrial Age businesses model which has been our heritage, backbone, and source of economic expansion since the U.S. was first established will be fully replaced by a developing and still unproven Connected Age businesses model. This business model paradigm shift will either be the most exciting or frightful reality Millennials create during their tenure in the workplace.

Millennial unleashing must be directed toward identifying and completing business model paradigm shifts for those companies that will transform into the Connected Age. In the not too distant past one-time massive businesses - Kodak, Blockbusters, and Borders Books, for example, disappeared due to technological advances which totally disrupted their business models. Now imagine major artificial intelligence (AI) advances on the near-term horizon that radically impact all technologies and business models. Millennials will be making the front-line informed decisions of which Industrial Age businesses will not make

Going Through A Millennium Change Cycle (MCC)

the transformation and go the way of the dinosaurs by as early as 2025. If you are interested in your company making the transformation, get your Millennials started working on the problem.

Mark Cuban of "Shark Tank" fame and owner of the Dallas Mavericks has had a lot to say about the coming changes in the workplace and culture in general related to the Connected Age. Specifically, he has addressed on multiple occasions drastic changes coming due to the introduction of AI at the local level. "Artificial Intelligence, deep learning, machine learning — whatever you're doing if you don't understand it — learn it. Because otherwise you're going to be a dinosaur within 3 years."[3] "Literally, who you work for, how you work, the type of work you do is going to be completely different than your parents within the next 10 to 15 years,"[4] Cuban says. "Even if you have no interest in computers, no interest in programming, it doesn't matter. Just like you laugh at your parents who might or might not understand Snapchat and Instagram and Twitter and the like, you are going to have to understand AI or people are going to laugh at you."[5] Notice what Cuban said about work in the next 10 to 15 years, the effects of the MCC are here.

History shows that the generations that get us into a mess are rarely the ones who rescue us from their mistakes. Thank goodness we don't have to worry about who will get us out of this one. They are already here—the Millennials. Before you snicker or laugh out loud let me note that appropriately named Millennials have been patiently, and at times frustratedly, awaiting recognition, empowerment, and assimilation into the workplace where they fully deserve to be. They will quickly, if not already, occupy significant positions in all workplace environments.

Millennials are the generation born between 1982 and 2000. In 2020, they are between twenty to thirty-eight years old and are a numerous group—between seventy to one-hundred million in the U.S. alone, depending on demographic data. It is the most educated generation in human history. Their relational and innovative mindset is well ingrained in their psyche. They have the unique ability to communicate, cooperate, collaborate, and co-create (C4) on a global level. Using technology, they can spur creativity and innovation to new heights. Prior generations in the 20th century developed particle physics and quantum mechanics, split the atom, discovered hyperspaces, and developed semi-conductors and computers. They took us to the moon and back, made dramatic discoveries in cosmology, mapped the human genome, discovered neuro-electrical biochemical pathways from which mind emerges in the prefrontal cortex of the brain, and rolled out the first iterations of AI. It is upon these foundational developments that the Millennials begin their own creativity, innovation, and discovery. Already, at the dawn of true globalization, scientists are synthesizing neurological discoveries with AI and seeing a future yet unknown. Millennials and their cadre of superstars will lead the way.

Millennials are no different from past generations regarding their willingness and ability to work hard and invest buckets of sweat equity. They do not feel a sense of entitlement and are certainly not confused. Millennials have been digitally trained and equipped to assess, envision, and creatively innovate marketable solutions to today's complex problems, far outstripping the abilities of older Gen-Xers (born between 1963 and 1981; 39 to 57-years old in 2020) and Boomers (born between 1946 and 1962; 58 to 74-years old in 2020).

Today's technology was envisioned, developed, and introduced to the market by older generations in the workplace who built upon what prior generations had accomplished. Similarly, Millennials will take today's technology to an entirely new level as their vision extends to horizons beyond the sight of a seasoned workforce. They have been specially prepared for this purpose and are ready now, not later, to be unleashed from workplace environments that are stuck in the 1990s and allowed to create and innovate in workspaces of the 21st century.

One of the philosophic effects that keyed me in on the idea of a MCC was Millennials awakening collective consciousness to seek out and discover individual life meaning, purpose, and calling. This is significant and harkens back to the cultural attitude in Athens around the time of the birth of the Age of Western Philosophy in the 6th Century BCE. The beauty of their seeking is that meaning, purpose, and calling are philosophic concepts explored by the earliest of philosophers and experienced vocationally in engagement, productivity, and loyalty (EPL) respectively.

Beginning in the late 1990s and continuing into the 2000s, the MCC effect could be seen building in college and university campuses around the country. In the workplace, evidence of the incoming MCC began to appear around 2006. As increasing numbers of Millennials entered the

Going Through A Millennium Change Cycle (MCC)

workforce, their entry was not warmly greeted by Boomers but rather disparaged or, even worse, ignored. Millennials were openly ridiculed for not getting with the program of doing their job. Things began to change around 2014 when the Boomers lost their control of the narrative. Millennials began to articulate that they were not broken and did not need fixing. Instead, they made it clear that the Industrial Age workplace needed to be replaced by a Connected Age environment. Throughout this period as Millennials clamored for development, advancement, and work/life balance what they heard in response was merely crickets.

Boomers began hitting the sixty-five-year retirement threshold in 2011 about ten years after Millennials began to enter the workforce. Boomers went from being the most represented generation in the workplace to the least in 2016, yet they still hold many seats of expansive power over the workplace and workforce. This current hold on power could drastically change as Coronavirus infection worries may prevent many Boomers from ever returning to a busy workplace while contraction of the virus is still possible.

The MCC tsunami will crest and hit full force in the workplace around 2025 when Millennials will make-up seventy-five percent of the global workforce with only a few Boomers left to cross the retirement threshold by 2027. Without Boomers in the way, Millennial and Xer leaders will make the final business model shift and for some older Xers and Boomers it will be a very hard shift. Development, advancement, and work/life balance will be on-going routine functions woven into the fabric of every workplace culture.

Between now and 2025, with real demands for creativity and innovation in organizations of all sizes, massive amounts of critical institutional knowledge (IK) that could be captured and/or innovated will continue to simply walk out the door as key personnel retire. Unleash Millennials to gather, create and innovate valuable and irreplaceable IK before it vanishes forever as Boomers walk out the door to retire.

We've heard a lot about Millennials and Boomers, but what about the in-between generation of Xers? Let me repeat two earlier lines in this chapter as they are significant and relevant to this question. Millennials make up fifty percent of the U.S. workforce[6] and Ernst & Young and Accenture are reporting that seventy-five percent of their workforces are already Millennial.[7] Where are the Xers in the workplace that would be expected to significantly reduce the Millennial percentages, especially in 2020? I'll address this in an entire chapter devoted to Xers, but the short answer is the Xers you're thinking should be in the workplace were never born, not here in the U.S. anyway. This is a huge issue and is deserving of an entire chapter.

The aftermath of the MCC tsunami will not be resolved until a new philosophical age is developed, a topic for another book. Millennials are ready to be Unleashed now in development, advancement, and work/life balance and are fully capable of creating change needed to Save the World. Key to Millennial Unleashing is the recovery of philosophic truth in the workplace and guiding the final transformation of Connected Age businesses. With the last of the Boomers quickly transitioning out of the workplace there is little time to delay.

We will begin our journey in Chapter 2 with a brief story specifically devoted to Boomers and Xers—What happened while we were sleeping? How did a MCC tsunami arise without our realizing it? Chapters 3 and 4 will go into more detail about Boomers and Xers, each in turn. We'll next look at what is called "work" in Chapter 5 and explore why that idea needs to be updated. The MCC tsunami and resulting millennium change will be introduced in Chapter 6 followed by chapters devoted the MCC precipitating "Age" shifts. The philosophic "Age" shift is a stand-alone in Chapter 7. The business model paradigm "Age" shift is broken up into three chapters: Chapter 8-economic, Chapter 9-technologic, and Chapter 10-pedagogic.

With all this as background, in Chapter 11 we'll dive deep into exploring the Millennials, the greatest generation in history, and discover what makes them tick. What is coaching and why it is the best practices method for Millennial learning is the topic of Chapter 12. Individual chapters on engagement, productivity, and loyalty and their drivers are presented as Chapters 13 to 15.

We take a brief reprieve in Chapter 16 and 17. Chapter 16 reveals to Millennials the Boomer paradigm of not knowing there was life meaning, purpose, or calling. Chapter 17 reveals in story form why a paradigm differential is valid and why Millennials have the correct paradigm to address what is ahead of us. Hopefully, these two chapters will help bridge some of the generational tensions in the workplace.

Going Through A Millennium Change Cycle (MCC)

An EPL Coaching program is presented in Chapter 18 that I have used to empower Millennials for alignment, development, and advancement along a career path while enhancing their engagement productivity, and loyalty. Coaching is the gateway to rapid creativity and innovation in workplaces of all Ages. This is followed up by Chapter 19 which presents concepts and six examples of how to implement multiple coaching accelerants to Unleash Millennial EPL for rapid and sustainable innovation in the workplace. These concepts and examples for Unleashing Millennials include: Creativity and Innovation Catalysts; Leadership Optimization; Succession Implementation; Institutional Knowledge Transfer; Next Generation Leader Development; and Millennial Dream Team Formation.

Chapter 20 examines how we can recapture in the workplace truth and knowability away from Postmodern skepticism about anything being true or knowable. This is a critical step to ensure we survive in a world awash in relativism.

The book concludes with a brief look in Chapter 21 at what we may be experiencing as Millennials gain control of all aspects of global leadership shortly after 2025. Will anyone alive today remember in 2040 what it was like in the stone ages back in 2020. If you can remember where we've come since Y2K multiply that exponentially and you may still not be close to the changes the world is about to experience.

Millennials have a great opportunity to discover their life meaning, to accomplish their purpose in the world for which they were created, and to demonstrate in-mass vocational loyalty as they develop, advance, and achieve work/life balance in the workplace. My hope is that in the process of advancement they recapture philosophic truth and fully transition viable businesses into the Connected Age. Our future is in their hands; and I for one am very excited about what they may accomplish.

The time for Unleashing Millennials within existing organizations may be short. They are gritty and vision-driven and no longer waiting to be Unleashed. They are already casting aside their shackles within dying companies that blindly cling to the Industrial Age business model and beginning a torrential entrance into the cycle of creativity and innovation in Connected Age businesses of their own. Only time will tell if their entrepreneurial choice results in their disrupting and replacing many existing businesses. Let's get started.

Unleash The Millennials and Save the World

In the next chapter we'll encounter a short allegory illustrating for all generations the significance of the paradigm shift in the current business model and how it was initially viewed in the Boomer dominated workplace. Get your hat, shades, and sunscreen ready as we step on a once peaceful beach where the Industrial Age Boomers experience first-hand what it is like to be faced with the Connected Age millennium change cycle (MCC) tsunami approaching. Unleash The Millennials and Save the World.

CHAPTER 2

While We Were Sleeping | A Boomer & Xer Story

This chapter tells a story about why Boomers and Xers woke up from a dream-state sometime just after 2011 and realized everything in the workplace had suddenly changed. It was not like we hadn't been working feverishly since we took our first jobs. Almost overnight it seemed everything changed. From the way we hired, trained, and advanced good talent and fired those who were disengaged. The change included new demands for work/life balance, new technologies of every description, concerns about our health and fitness, and the health of the planet due to climate change. We went from one day making and doing things to meet a market demand to the next day being required to make and do things that were renewable, sustainable, left a low carbon footprint, and still met the market demands we faced the day before. We went from one day having a pretty good idea of how everyone thought and talked about things in the workplace to the next day having no idea if something we said was, in fact, offensive, and now we would be held accountable or even fired.

Here we are nine years later having learned to adjust and function somewhat within the new paradigm which will continue for the foreseeable future. Something really did happen while we were working which will be described in greater detail in the next few chapters. I just wanted to take this opportunity to remind the Boomer readers, and let the Millennials know where Boomers and to a lesser extent Xers are coming from. In hindsight, I'd say that waking up was good for all of us and actually brought into the workplace what we've always yearned for but never had—intentional professional development, career path advancement, and work/life balance. I use a dream metaphor and story to set the stage and then provide the reality of our dream in the workplace.

When Millennials were first being born (1982) Boomers were entering their full stride in the workplace and Xers were just a few years shy of entering the workforce. For Boomers, work was life and in the 1980s our lives greatly improved during the longest period of economic expansion in our history as stated in a 1990 article in The New York Times:

> We don't know whether historians will call it the Great Expansion of the 1980s or Reagan's Great Expansion, but we do know from official economic statistics that the seven-year period from 1982 to 1989 was the greatest, consistent burst of economic activity ever seen in the U.S. In fact, it was the greatest economic expansion the world has ever seen—in any country, at any time.[8]

While we worked hard before, during, and after this expansion we also went to sleep while working, and this was our dream. We found ourselves riding this economic cresting wave for all it was worth and soon the Xers joined us and together we productively surfed in and out of the cresting pipeline. As the wave began to close upon itself, we all jumped off our boards and into the water and began paddling out to catch the next wave. But something unexpected happened while we paddled out—successive waves diminishing in size and intensity. Soon, the beach was being struck by nothing but small swales breaking near us. By the time half of the Xers had joined us we had given up our surfboards for productivity boogie boards to ride the swales. When the last of the Xers arrived, we had finally settled on productivity skim boards along the beach as the water had become relatively flat. With each successive adjustment in boards we all had to work that much harder to experience even a fraction of the ease and thrill of the systems of production we had just abandoned.

Sometime in early 2005, as the Boomers and Xers were skim boarding along the beach, we could see on the horizon through our binoculars a huge wave approaching with what looked like skipping sailboats. The closer the wave got, the easier it was to distinguish that rather than skipping sailboats people were riding something like small surfboards with a sail attached. As the wave got a little closer, the younger-Xers began to get all excited as they recognized they were Millennials and said, "They must be windsurfing." We all just stood with our mouths open, gawking at the approaching marvel of surfing (aka production innovation).

Soon a group of Millennials walked from the parking area behind us and asked if they could help us with our work? We gave them some skim boards and told them to get to it. They just stared at us. A couple of us tossed our boards into the lapping water and demonstrated what they were to do and told them to give it a try. A few Millennials just left, a couple more gave it a try and then sat on the beach staring at the approaching wave and riders, while the rest joined in and laboriously continued until they mastered the skim boarding productivity glide.

It wasn't long after the Millennials began to show up that a Xer and an older Millennial grabbed one of our old surfboards out of storage, attached a mast on a ball swivel and a small sail. While we skim boarded, the Xer helped the Millennial get the awkward contraption to the water and steadied him while he let the sail fill with wind and windsurfing productivity on our beach began. It was hard work for them to stay on the board and maneuver the sail, but they eventually got where they could keep it in a straight line and get productive windsurfing accomplished.

We Boomers laughed at them, telling the other Xers and Millennials of the 1980s when we surf boarded the pipeline for maximum surfing productivity. Now that was real work, real fun, and real productivity. To get the crew ready to greet the approaching wave and riders we let a few other Xer and Millennial teams make additional windsurfing boards so they could continue to test and refine the new productivity concept. We demanded that the rest continue productively skim boarding.

Millennials kept showing up at the beach while the incoming wave and riders steadily approached. Our windsurfing-testing routine lasted until 2011 when the oldest of the Boomers began to retire and relocate to a Margaritaville -type community. Shortly thereafter, several busloads of Millennials showed up with a tractor trailer following behind. As they approached the beach, we noticed they were all carrying what looked like modified waterskiing wake boards and backpacks. We laughed at them and told them what our "skim" board work required. They laughed louder

Unleash The Millennials and Save the World

back at us and said, "That's what we've come to do," pointing to the wave riders still at a distance. We told them, "We're doing the same thing, you'll just have to wait your turn," as we pointed to our windsurfing test group. That only made them laugh louder as they began to yell out to the test teams in the flat water to come in and be shown how to literally fly surfing.

We didn't like that and told them to start skimming. Some of the new Millennials started skimming, some didn't, and some began to talk with the younger Xers on the beach and the test teams as they came in. The new Millennials explained that they had innovated the absolute pinnacle of surfing productivity by combining windsurfing and wakeboarding. They noted the wave we saw with riders approaching was a millennium change cycle (MCC) tsunami and the riders were not windsurfing but rather kitesurfing. Kitesurfing involved surfers on modified wakeboards and literally harnessed at the hip to an acrobatic parachute similar to what stunt skydivers use. With a wakeboarding tow rope like handle attached to the ends of the parasail, skilled hands and a quick mind allows kitesurfers to rip and literally fly across the water. Surf productivity they said was over the top and was outcome-based and not on how many skim runs were made.

We didn't buy it and before long most of them needed the work, so they began skimming. A couple of the grittier new Millennials who had been sitting on the beach opened their backpacks. They were undeterred by our refusal to allow anything beyond skim boarding. They harnessed themselves to their boards, deployed their sails, and positioned them directly overhead just idling in the wind. It didn't take long for some edgy creative and innovative Boomers and Xers to surround the Millennials and a raucous conversation ensued with much laughing and guffawing by all. Scott, our best and brightest Boomer in the group asked to take a try at it. Initially the Millennials recommended a little coaching and training but soon stopped. They saw by his reaction that Scott wasn't an instruction reader and didn't like outside assistance.

As he was being strapped in, Scott said to his gathered peers, "If I can't figure this out on the first try, it can't be done." After he had motioned to the Millennial holding the sail to let it fly, he may have regretted what came next. Scott was dragged with board securely attached nearly a hundred yards down the beach before the Millennial caught up and collapsed the sail. The entire little band of blow-offs (i.e. a term of endearment we skim boarders gave all slackers) ran all the way laughing and whooping to the beached whale, Scott.

Scott slowly and painfully released his feet from the board boots and lay on the beach laughing and crying at the same time. "That was so awesome, but I really could have done without the sand burn!" We seasoned skim boarders thought Scott got what he deserved; play with fire and you'll get burned.

Next, we saw Cindy, our brightest Xer, putting on everything just taken off of Scott. The new Millennial who had lent Scott his equipment asked Cindy if she'd like some instruction. She very kindly declined and pointed out the wave of riders and said, "My little brother is out there, and we learned to kitesurf together." Cindy then asked Scott to stand next to her as she needed to speak to him privately. After a short-muffled conversation, Scott stepped back smiling and said, "If you can do what you say, I'll back you all the way."

When the Millennial launched Cindy's sail it started to pull her over as it had Scott, earlier, but swish-swish she worked the control handle and, lickety split, the sail soon positioned itself overhead and idled. Cindy took a deep breath and gave a quick and smooth pull on the tow handle and like a bullet launched off the beach.

It wasn't long before her flying took her out over the water. As she quickly descended and with just the slightest lift, she raised the board up just before hitting the water. She took off like a wakeboarder in full lean on the edge. It wasn't long before Cindy began to skip and fly like the wave riders on the wave now in clear view. After a few minutes of a great show on the water she made her way back to the now crowded beach of onlookers.

As she beached her board and idled the sail, she then unstrapped from the board, pulled the harness release, and the sail floated harmlessly to the beach a few yards away. Cindy and Scott immediately walked off the beach together as a crowd of Millennials and younger Xers followed.

We shouted to all our beach skimmers to get back to it, as we had to meet real skimming quotas before the work was done. We also let it be known that any of our beach skimmers who didn't come back immediately didn't need to worry about coming back later as they were fired. Although we had just witnessed one of our own perform amazing surf productivity kitesurfing, pretty soon we just got back to work because that is what we did.

A couple of weeks later a convoy of buses and trucks parked down the beach from where we were skimming and unloaded new Millennials with boards and backpacks. As soon as they had donned their gear, each was off into the water kitesurfing and creating surf productivity numbers off the chart.

When the skyline began to fill with kitesurfers, we noticed Scott and Cindy making their way to us from that direction. Scott was always direct and didn't waste any words. He explained how he had devoted his whole life to a vocation of surfing, and while skim boarding helped pay the bills, kitesurfing productivity was far superior to even our pipeline surfboarding business almost 40-years ago. He had bankrolled a new surfing business, "KiteKare," and made Cindy the CEO. Cindy spoke next and was not so brief as Scott, but I'll keep it brief here.

Cindy noted to us that the riders we saw coming toward shore are riding a MCC tsunami wave that will, in short order, completely swamp us. The KiteKare surfers now on the water will simply fly up and join the others on the wave as it approaches the beach. In face of that reality, do we want to: 1) Merge with KiteKare or sell our skim boarding business to them? 2) Bankroll our own transformation into a KiteKare type business model if time allows? 3) Continue to operate as a skim boarding business and be buried by KiteKare's massive surfing productivity advantage, or 4) Be totally wiped-out when the MCC tsunami hits?

We never answered, as the freight of what we could clearly see in our dream woke us up from this nightmare sometime after 2011. Millennials, to be sure, were a true nightmare to many Boomers as they entered the work force. They thought and acted with defiant indifference to our expectation to "just be quiet and do as you're told."

In the next chapter, Millennial readers will see what we Boomers endured growing up and throughout our careers. We hope it is clear that Boomers desired to spare younger generations our same experience, thus we raised them differently to be exactly who they are today—bright, inquisitive, intuitive, creative, and innovative. We want Millennials to take the future in their hands and run with it. Boomers now is the time to experience the fruit of our labor in preparing our children for such a time as this; Unleash The Millennials and Save the World.

CHAPTER 3

Who Are Boomers? | Oldest Generation in Workforce

Boomers (born between 1946 and 1962; 58 to 74-years old in 2020) entered the workforce around 1964 when the oldest Boomers started to turn 18. Boomers were a large generation (80 million) that followed after the smaller Silent Generation (55 million). Not all Boomers went to college, as a high school degree at that time opened doors to many Industrial Age work opportunities. Opportunities in a country setting were predominantly agricultural, while in the city, opportunities abounded in many relatively well-paying trade crafts, industrial production, and manufacturing jobs. And for many Boomers, starting a job after high school was not an option as they were either drafted or volunteered for military duty during the Vietnam War. By the early 1970s and the end of the Vietnam conflict, Boomers began entering the workforce in masse and continued to do so until around 1980 when the youngest Boomers were around eighteen years old.

The Boomers entering the workforce were predominantly male initially as many Boomer women were still expected to align with the traditional role of getting married and becoming a stay-at-home mom. Very few opportunities were open to Boomer women who wished to have careers. By the early 1970s the percentage of Boomer women entering the workforce increased significantly as opportunities in nearly all sectors of business and industry continued growing steadily. Soon two working parent households became the norm (among whites, at least) and the disposable family income increased dramatically over prior generations.

Unleash The Millennials and Save the World

Philosophically, Boomers were raised as modern thinkers (to be more fully defined later) who had a sense that science ruled the world of knowledge and life, and the way in life was pretty straightforward. There were physical laws in effect that dictated a norm of the cosmos; psychological profiles that dictated the norms of behavior; and federal, state, and local laws that dictated how to live together. The Boomer's role, philosophically, was to live what was viewed as a responsible and respectable life: get an education, get a job, get married, have a family, buy a house, work and save till you're sixty-five, retire, and enjoy any grandchildren that come along. There was not a sense of individual life purpose; you simply did as you were told and went to work whether you liked what you did or not.

At the time Boomers were growing up (1946 to early 1970s), the majority in the U.S. were raised in Christian households and attended church with their families regularly. During this time, Boomers faced a confusing dualism. You went to church on Sunday and learned about a spiritual life and then switched your brain to live absent of a spiritual influence at work Monday to Saturday. This dualism of faith and secular life held its ground in the Boomers until the mid-1970s when the effects of the philosophical shift from Modern Philosophy to our current Postmodern period began to be fully experienced culturally.

Modern philosophical thinking was science-based and materialistic (i.e. all that exists is physical). Spiritual thought was believed by many modern thinkers, including many in mainline denominational churches, to have been an evolutionary artifact of myths used to explain natural phenomena. The shift to Postmodernism, which is based in a belief essentially atheistic (i.e. not rooted in any theology), allowed increasing numbers of individual Boomers to abandon their Sunday religious obligations and just live life as they best saw fit, which many did in droves.

The Boomers who were raised in a religious culture made their move into a more secular culture following a series of upheavals that began in the mid-1950s and continued until the early 1970s. The first upheaval was in 1955 in Alabama where there was a righteous push back within the black community against racial segregation laws. The ugliness of racism made world news when peaceful desegregation marches were met with murders that fomented riots across the South. In 1962, the U.S. Supreme Court deemed school prayer unconstitutional. In 1963, a beloved president, John F. Kennedy, was assassinated in Dallas. In 1965, the U.S. Supreme Court deemed it legal for couples to use the birth control pill. In the mid-1960s, demonstrations against U.S. involvement in the Vietnam War began in earnest across the country with two mantras "Make love not war" and, "Sex, drugs, and rock & roll." The peace symbol, long hair for men, and hippie style dress made an entrance into daily life as well as an aboveground drug culture on college campuses. In 1968, the civil rights leader Martin Luther King, Jr. was assassinated as was the nation's Attorney General, Robert F. Kennedy. In 1970, four students were killed and nine more wounded as Ohio National Guard forces opened fire on a group of unarmed college students protesting the war at Kent State University. And in 1973, the Supreme Court legalized abortion, protecting women's reproductive rights.

Almost the entire Boomer generation was raised and began entering the workforce during this time of upheaval. These upheavals caused significant changes in social behavior and subsequently laws that reflected this new behavior. An example would be that, at one time, most of the nation had what were called blue laws that did not allow commerce on Sundays. Nothing was open except for drug stores and gas stations, and typically only prescription drugs and gas were allowed to be sold. Alcohol was not sold on Sundays! Sundays were quiet days as most were in church with nothing happening culturally with the exception of professional sports. By the early 1970s the blue laws became history, by the early 1980s you could buy alcohol on Sundays, and by the late 1980s Sunday was like any other day.

Not only did the blue laws change but the family structure changed as well. Even up until the mid-1970s in a high school of 1600 students, it was rare for a student's parents to divorce. Rarely did a classmate get pregnant and if they did most didn't know about it as the student was moved from the school and possibly the community. Homosexuality and adultery were illegal, and it was difficult to get a divorce, especially if you were a woman. Of course, all this changed radically in a little under twenty years.

While there was much social upheaval all about, all Boomers entered an Industrial Age workplace for which they were all prepared. Their rows and columns education and top down authority structure reinforced by swats in school by the principal made life at work very understandable.

Unleash The Millennials and Save the World

You did what you were told at the place you were assigned and didn't make trouble. Rarely were group tasks assigned, but if it was, each person was held responsible for his or her own work.

The economy was growing and opportunities for advancement abounded and Boomers took advantage. Soon Boomers found themselves saddled with tremendous responsibilities on critical work assignments before the age of 30. They handled it all in stride and rode the waves quickly to the top of organizational managerial pyramids. By the mid-1970s many were well beyond where they thought they'd be and discovered the sex, drugs, and rock and roll they learned about in college had also been flowing freely in the workplace for many years.

It seems so strange to write all this and realize how messed up we Boomers were in comparison to today, even before we entered the workforce. Seat belts in a car were ornamental and there were no headrests up until 1968! Color television was not introduced until the mid-1960s. Homes were small and modest, many families had only one car, two at the most, and vacations were spent in small simple hotels with beds and a pool. And for the drive to the vacation spot you packed your own lunch as there were no fast food restaurants. Bathroom, soft drinks, and peanuts at the gas station and back on the road.

Well over a third if not more of the population smoked heavily, and smoking was allowed in all public spaces. Drinking was something you started as soon as you could pick up a beer can or cocktail glass off your parents' table. If you were pulled over for driving while intoxicated the cop called someone to give you a ride home or they took you there themselves. This lifestyle, which seems abhorrent today, was a regular part of the culture white Boomers were raised in at home and at work.

Two-martini lunches were not uncommon in the workplace when Boomers showed up. Or better yet, drinking at work was not uncommon in some settings. Boomers learned that liquor at work was acceptable as long as it was presented in fashionable decanters. We were told by the older generation that it helped to get the creative juices going. Just watch some office drama movies from the late 1950s and early 1960s and you'll see the workplaces we entered.

Throughout the boom of the 1980s, Boomers were high on themselves and their successes. Two-worker Boomer households were flush with cash, which they spent. And what cash we didn't have we just created magically by using credit cards. It was at this time we began having kids (i.e. the Millennials). As the culture shifted with the collapse of the Modern Philosophy and end of 2600-years of Western Philosophy as we know it, we also began transforming business model paradigms from the Industrial Age to the Connected Age and the wheels of our party bus began to come off. It was a perfect storm when Western Philosophy and our business model paradigm shifted together.

The social upheavals of the 1960s and early 1970s made it very easy for Boomers to disregard the authoritative top-down Modern Philosophy science model that had all the answers we'd been raised on. We could plainly see we were killing ourselves with smoking and drinking, our personal relationships were all askew, and we had to stop hating each other for just being different. So, when Postmodernism rolled in and said there is no God although you can believe in myths if you want, you can do what you want, and stop judging others for being different, we adopted it. Not that we knew what the consequences of such a thinking would be, we just knew there had to be a change from the messed-up social culture we inherited from our parents. And we were not going to raise our kids the way we were raised; and we didn't.

By the end of the 1980s, divorce, single-parent homes, blended families, and the reality of latch-key kids became more common among Boomers. While we worried about this, changes in the workplace required we put our home worries on hold. Computers that had entered the workplace in the early 1980s were now everywhere. While we tried to keep up with the latest software, new more robust hardware kept rolling in with even more complicated software, eventually including networking and servers. Orders for our industrial products and manufacturing goods began to fall as competition from foreign markets rose.

Then the 1970s gas-crisis hit, and the U.S. automakers fumbled badly with cheaply made, ugly, and poor performing clunkers that opened the door to foreign imports in every sector of the manufacturing market imaginable. Before the gas crisis, you could buy a basic U.S. built car but to get options you had to pay extra. And most Boomers knew not to buy a U.S. car that was built on a Monday or the day following a holiday, or it would be a lemon. This reality resulted in the passage of lemon laws in numerous states. After the crisis was resolved with high gas prices remaining, you could go to an import dealer (I remember initially only

Unleash The Millennials and Save the World

Honda) and buy a small fuel-efficient car for about half the base model price of a fuel inefficient U.S. clunker. Soon, it wasn't just foreign cars we were buying but almost every technology-based manufactured good you can imagine from stereo systems and televisions to washing machines and copiers were made overseas.

If that wasn't bad enough, the Internet appeared and suddenly we had to not just compete against our neighbor down the street but competition from around the country began to appear on our customers' screens with a few clicks of a button. We had to work doubly hard to keep the work we could get locally while joining the fray to chase work nationally and internationally. And wouldn't you know it, the rest of the world found out how to sell to us via the Internet. They were now creating products themselves in plants relocated to their countries to avoid new stringent U.S. environmental standards and access cheap labor. Industrial production and manufacturing plummeted, putting many Boomers out of work or requiring them to change careers.

Soon Boomers were no longer capable of handling all the technological and positional changes at work and simply became very narrow in their vocational focus. We were raised to do everything ourselves with no help or teamwork. Entirely new types of workers (Xers) began entering the workforce to address new areas of workplace engagement such as Information Technology (IT) and Human Resources (HR). To keep up, Boomers just kept their heads down and worked harder not to make waves.

As all this was going on, Boomers blindly abandoned their kids to an education system that was totally enmeshed in Postmodernism. While the materialism of science was retained (i.e. everything is physical), the direction of education was on social reform with an extreme skepticism of truth and knowability about any topic including history, science, math, literature, and government. Over time public education opened the door to a new world for the Millennials. This new direction in pedagogy was in a technology-based framework to prepare students to work in a global technology-based economy with no nationalistic boarders. Millennials are the first global citizens in a one world system yet to be established.

While they knew their Millennial kids were thinking in a new way, Boomers were too busy at work to deal with them. So, they would give them $100 dollars to go to the mall and not get in trouble while they

Who Are Boomers? | Oldest Generation in Workforce

worked. They thought giving children a bigger house, a car, a cell phone, and lots of cash would keep them quiet until we had time for some "quality time" with them. That quality time would happen on expensive vacations, but really all that happened was parents worked and gave the kids some cash to spend.

In the early 1990s, Boomers figured it out—they were messing up the kids. Next, the plan was to raise Millennial kids giving them everything Boomers had missed growing up. Parents loved and doted on their children and ensured they were educated—not to get a job but to discover their life purpose. In fact, we in essence paid our kids with cash, credit cards, cell phones, cars, apartments, college tuitions, etc. not to stay out of trouble but so they could learn and grow and have the freedom to become well-rounded emotionally and pursue their passions. We all knew they would do amazing things with our generous support.

I noted earlier that many Boomers upon graduation from high school went to work in relatively well-paying trade crafts or in industrial or manufacturing jobs. This was partly because of opportunity and to a significant extent because not all parents had the financial resources to send their children to college. Boomers, from their beginning in the workplace, had a mindset that college was not optional for their kids; they would go to college whether their mom and dad had gone or not. Many saved for this while others hoped their kids could earn a scholarship, take advantage of grants, and/or borrow money for their college education.

A significant downturn in industrial production and manufacturing at the time many Millennials were graduating from high school also made college a good choice. It was not uncommon for employers to require college degrees for minimum wage, entry level positions. Suddenly college was no longer optional, but necessary.

Finally, around 2004, Millennials began to show up for work ready to start careers. They didn't smoke, drink, or fool around; they just wanted to know what needed to be done so they could do it. We'd tell them to sit at a desk and gave them some entry work to get them started. Soon they were back in our office wanting to know the big picture and how they could be involved. Oh no! They wanted our jobs! They were faster, smarter, and more tech savvy with zero experience than we were with our thirty years of experience. And if we boiled down what we really knew in our narrow vocational focus it became evident they could pick that up in

Unleash The Millennials and Save the World

a couple of weeks; so, we parked them where they were. We didn't communicate, certainly didn't cooperate, and never imagined collaborating or co-creating with them to innovate anything.

The Boomer philosophy in the Industrial Age business model paradigm has been and still is to keep doing what we've been doing until we can retire and then you Xers and Millennials can have it. And while many Boomers have joined Connected Age businesses, they are still operating with an Industrial Age mindset toward their Millennial workers.

Boomers – WAKE UP! It is fully on your shoulders to unleash the Millennial talent we raised and coach them in truth and knowability through open communication, cooperation, collaboration, and co-creation (C4) so they can create and innovate workplace solutions that address increasingly vast and complex global business issues.

With Boomers now fully uncovered and undone, it is time to address those missing Xers in the workforce. This is perhaps one of the most critical near-term crises in the workplace today, pushing us even harder to Unleash The Millennials and Save the World.

CHAPTER 4

Where Are Missing Xers? | They were never BORN!

Now it is time to unveil one of the scariest realities in the workplace when considering the rapid rate of Boomers retiring. And for this act of the play, Xers are the stars of the show.

Xers were born between 1963 and 1981 and are between 39 and 57-years old in 2020. Demographically they are about half the size (45 million) of the Boomers above and the Millennials below them. Following this chapter and moving forward throughout the remainder of the book I will infrequently refer to the Xers (although this chapter is devoted to them).

Xers are sometimes termed the orphaned and forgotten generation because of how few of them there are compared to Boomers and Millennials. They are the generation of entrepreneurs whose best and brightest always had difficulty finding advancement within Boomer-dominated businesses. So rather than fight for positions that were not available, they started their own companies, many very successfully.

They were born and grew up in the middle of the aforementioned shifts. As a result, multiple surveys of Xers reveal they do not exhibit a unique generational identity, but rather exhibit characteristics in the workplace similar to Boomers or Millennials, or a combination. Rather than treat them after this chapter as a separate generation, it makes more sense to let them bleed into whatever bordering generation they feel most comfortable identifying with. While doing so may appear as a slight, I am confident that, as the book continues, Xers will identify with either Boomers or Millennials, both of which have stark differences in social, cultural, and workplace ideals. Or perhaps they will see elements of themselves on both sides of the aisle.

The Boomer and Millennial generations are large demographically (about 80 million plus each) with the in-between Xers only half their size (about 45 million). This hourglass demographic profile, with bulges at each end and not much in the middle, is creating a crisis in the workplace. There are not enough Xers in the workforce to replace all the Boomers who have retired or will be retiring. Half the Boomers are already sixty-five years old in 2020 with the last of the Boomers crossing that marker by 2027. We are currently at the point where there will be few, if any, Xers to replace retiring Boomers moving forward. Xers are already working in Boomer vacated spots. See the graphic below.

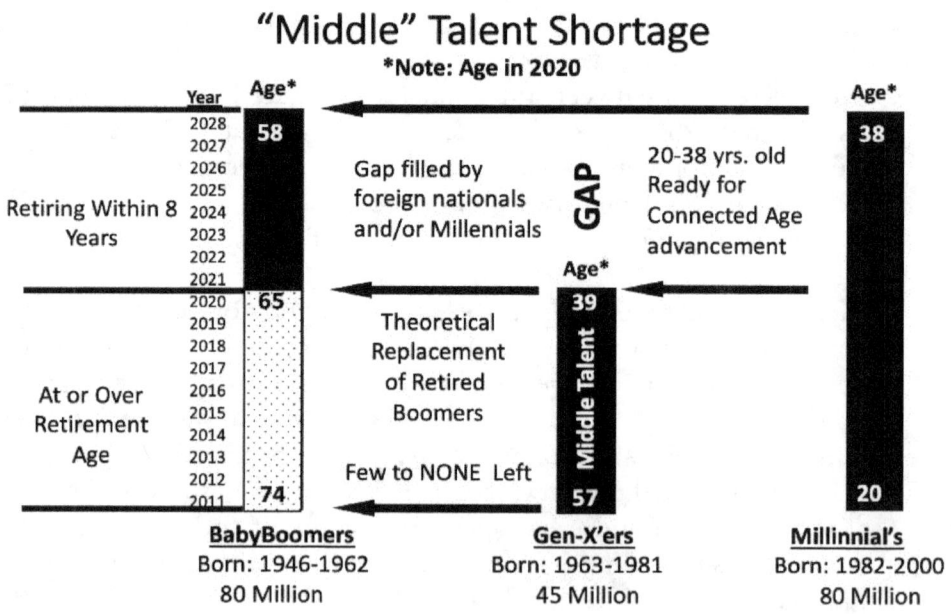

For over nine years this missing middle Xer generation has prompted U.S. businesses to recruit and hire from overseas to fill the recently vacated Xer positions. Thus, the necessity to hire experienced foreign

Where Are Missing Xers? | They were never BORN!

nationals to fill openings in every sector of our economy. Our workplaces are not only multicultural but increasingly becoming multi-national.

In 2020, there are only a few more Xers left to fill whatever vacancies Boomers make in the workplace at any level. And the extent of loss of Boomers returning to the workplace post pandemic is not yet know. This number may be significant. In the face of this, no matter what we do, we will not be able to (legally) bring enough experienced Xer talent from abroad into vacated positions within the next two years. Technological efficiency may take some of the load, but the rest of the Boomer vacated positions must be given to Millennial talent—ready or not. My suggestion is to Unleash The Millennials and provide them with ramped-up professional development aligned with career path openings that will occur within the next five years. There really is no other option.

What all this means is simple. At your next staff meeting, look around and see how many are 58 and over (Boomers) and 38 and under (Millennials). Then note how many Xers you have in between. Who in your organization (Xer and Millennial) is qualified, trained, and ready to replace all those Boomers who did not return post pandemic or will be retiring in five years? Who in your organization is qualified, trained, and ready to replace the Xer or Millennial who just replaced the Boomer? Millennials pay attention here. Many Boomers don't care what happens to the company after they leave or retire so they will do nothing to get you ready. If you plan on staying in a business like that, let them know that their doing nothing is unacceptable.

This crisis won't hit people until they realize that the lack of U.S.-born Xers in a particular vocation is not because of a preference for one vocation over another. The ones you're looking for were never born; they are not here. The U.S. has been giving Visas to a lot of Xers born in other countries to help fill the void, but we are nowhere close to filling the gap entirely. Possible reasons for this smaller U.S. Xer generation may include the Vietnam War, legalization of the birth control pill, and legalization of abortion all of which occurred within the Xer demographic birth window. Whatever the reason it really doesn't matter, the reality is, U.S. born Xers are a small generation bounded by two large generations.

I have a friend who works for a prestigious large national consulting firm and when I mentioned this hourglass reality, he gave me a look and the story behind the look. He said they were trying to hire an account

Unleash The Millennials and Save the World

executive with fifteen to twenty years of experience to handle work that demanded that level of experience. They tried local and regional job postings and literally got no responses for three months. He said they made a ridiculous salary and benefits offer and posted the opening nationally and did not get a single qualified response for six months. Finally, they had to hire a consultant in India to take over the accounts. He noted to me they were not being super selective; it was that no qualified Xers applied to fill the openings.

The second effect in the workplace due to the hourglass generational demographic is that many Millennials are having to report directly to Boomers. This two-generation accountability leap accentuates any normal differences in communications and relationships between successive generations. Boomers are managing talent of their own children's age and Millennials are reporting to people their parents age. The lack of communication and relationship because of the age gap and worldview change are real.

Many people remain ignorant of the dearth of Xers to fill middle management positions and replace retiring Boomers, and thus certainly are unaware of the dangers. There are many companies with great job openings that cannot find a field of qualified candidates to select from who are between 38 and 56 years old with 15 to 25 years of experience.

There is a solution to this Xer squeeze that involves ramping up vocational and leadership development and committing to nurture Xers and Millennials in their career paths to prepare sufficient coverage for Boomer vacancies that are on the horizon. Boomers reading this understand. Millennials reading this, what's coming is a time similar to when the Boomers entered the workforce; more opportunities for advancement than people to fill the seats—get ready!

What we will all learn together in this crisis is that work is much more than just a seat at a desk, a post at a station, or a means to a paycheck. Work is a central tenet of human existence for all generations and is intrinsically tied to life meaning, individual purpose, and vocational calling. Creativity and innovation in regard to engagement, productivity, and loyalty (EPL) are key to helping solve this missing Xer crisis. Xers have already stepped up and done their jobs, but their numbers are running low. Millennials, more than any other generation in the

Where Are Missing Xers? | They were never BORN!

workplace, are perfectly prepared to create and innovate EPL such that we blast beyond this crisis and into a bright future.

Speaking of work, that is the topic of our next chapter. In this chapter we will discover that while work itself has not changed, how work is viewed by Millennials in contrast to older generations in the workplace is significant. Millennials were raised to know their passions and they pursue work with passion in order to live a meaningful life. Unleash The Millennials and Save the World.

Unleash The Millennials and Save the World

CHAPTER 5

Work | Generational Differences are Significant

Work can be defined as any activity or effort, mental or physical, that is exerted in order to accomplish something. It is most simply acting purposefully for gain or to reach a goal as opposed to doing nothing, resting, or pursuing a leisure activity.

As Millennials began to enter the workforce, friction between generations in the workplace doing work sounded the alarm we were in for significant transformational change. The reason for the friction was primarily due to Millennials being incorrectly labeled early on in their entry to the workplace as an entitled generation averse to working in general. They've been described as wanting to exert only minimal energy to a task or mental exercise and being more interested in playing at life than working productively.

In reality, Millennials have the same internal human emotions and drives as other generations in the work force, and they do work, and work hard. As we'll see later, the big differentiator among "workers" in the workplace relates to how they were educated, the work environment they were prepared for, and what kind of work they were trained to do. The differences have caused massive disconnects between Boomers and Millennials because they were educated and trained differently for the same work to be done in almost completely different workplace environments.

Work has always marked our individual and collective contribution to the world regardless of any label of generation, class, gender, nationality, or ethnicity. Work provides life meaning, validates individual purpose, and affirms vocational calling. What this means is that work provides me assurance that my life is significant, validates that I have skills to create and innovate, and affirms that my ease in my position and love of what I do aligns with my vocational passion.

Millennials have a desire to experience and enjoy life in the now rather than spending their present moment "just working" with a hope of enjoyment at some future time—on a vacation or after retirement. This thought has been referred to as work/life balance and often disparaged or ridiculed by Boomers as just laziness or entitlement. The reality is that Boomer parents demonstrated to their own Millennial children that the reality of "just working" for the future is contrary to life harmony.

The Millennial children of Boomers saw that their parents' work choices produced stress, distress, anger, resentment, conflict, divorce, and many other personal, family, and social ills that cannot be easily overcome by a work-filled vacation. Boomer-raised children know that working hard 24/7 to earn money to buy things you don't need, to impress people you don't like, to pacify the kids you never see, and in the end crater the family dynamic is not something they want to repeat. Hallelujah!

Now here is why this perspective is crucial for Millennials. They are focused on meaning, purpose, and calling in all aspects of life, of which work is a part. They seek happiness in life both at work and away from work. Boomers also want that same happiness but are at times miserable because they cannot separate from work.

Older generations in the workplace (that includes me) were educated and entered into familiar and well-honed Industrial Age vocations and professions of work. Millennials were educated and prepared for entirely new Connected Age work possibilities while they were matriculating in school. The differences in almost every aspect of educational preparation for Industrial Age and Connected Age work are huge and continuing to diverge. This divergence in the workplace today is clearly seen in the Millennials top three drivers for engagement, productivity, and loyalty (EPL) which include vocational development, opportunities for advancement, and work/life balance. These are Millennial expectations they believe are necessary for them to do their work.

Older generations in the workplace had a sense on their first day work of "what" needed to be done because of our educational preparation. We

Work | Generational Differences are Significant

were taught in school not to ask "Why or How" things were done; we just got to it and did what we were trained to do. Not that these "Why and How" questions were forbidden, but they never came to mind. And if they did, the usual thought would have been a sense of prying into personal and/or trade secret types of information. Personal in the sense we were educated to do our own work and asking a neighbor the why and how they did their work was out of bounds. Trade secret type questions is the sense asking "Why and How" questions would be like asking for the recipe of Coca-Cola. "Why and How" type of questions about work had been answered by other people decades earlier we just did what we were told without questions.

Millennials were educated and prepared to work in Connected Age positions not yet known and which may have to be invented along the way. Part of their preparation for stepping into the unknown included being trained to always ask "Why and How" something is done; never assume you know. Part of the development Millennials are seeking in Industrial Age workplaces are simply the answers to two types of questions; 1) Why are they being asked to do what they are assigned?/Why is what is assigned important?; and 2) How should they accomplish the assignment?/How is this assigned work normally done? As will be discussed in more detail later, they were educated to occupy technology jobs to create and innovate upon jobs that were not even invented at the time they were in school.

The "Why" question is trying to find the motivational relevance for work being done. The Industrial Age answer of "Just because; now get back to work" makes no sense to a Millennial and is in fact an insult to their intelligence. There is certainly an answer, and the answer has direct relevance to whether this work will be continued in the Connected Age. That determination of relevance is found in the "How" question.

In a siloed Industrial Age workplace environment, "How" has little meaning as that was determined by prior generations and is typically outside the preview of the individuals doing the work. In a Connected Age Millennial workplace environment, "How" is a relational question that involves every avenue of possibility and personnel real and or imagined. Millennials are prepared for there not to be an immediate answer to "How" as perhaps they are the ones to invent it. "How" is the gateway door into creativity and innovation. If the how door is closed, work continues but with little or no advancement. Open the "How" door that allows Millennials to communicate, cooperate, collaborate, and co-create other ways to satisfy the motivations of the "Why." Creativity and innovation by definition and actuation alter in some manner the "How" of something already being done.

Older generations in the workplace had/have no need for personal vocational development beyond what was/is immediately needed in a position as work was/is "station" oriented and in done in vertical "silos" of activity. Industrial Age work was/is mechanical and/or machine like, well ordered, step by step, quantifiable, and honed to a fine edge of knowability. Opportunities for career path advancement for older generations in the workplace occurred when openings became available and were filled by qualified candidates. Everyone worked with little or no expectation of life outside of work while you were at work. Rest and leisure while recognized, were not considered integral parts of the Industrial Age workplace environment. Those were things you did when not working.

Vocational development for Millennials is all about answering the "Why and How" questions previously addressed. They know "What" to do in todays Connected Age far more then prior generations in the workplace. Millennials are highly tuned and prepared to evaluate motivations (i.e. "Why") and means (i.e. "How") and envision (i.e. "What") if there are more creative and innovative ways to accomplish the same thing. The nature of the Connected Age is such that likely nothing, and I mean nothing, in the analog Industrial Age will fully transition between Ages until the "Why and How" sieves are optimized in Connected Age terms.

Millennial career path advancement has been slow coming and is possibly related to older generations perception of institutional knowledge (IK). When openings occur the most qualified in terms of IK advance although much more technically qualified and proficient Millennial talent may be available. Access to IK is typically related to tenure, opportunities, and who you know. Problems occur when the IK holder is not qualified and proficient in the Connected Age business model. He or she may know a lot, but it is worth zero if they don't know what to do with it. Put a top Millennial talent in an advancement opening and they will discover and/or invent new IK if the institutions IK is withheld by older generation

Work | Generational Differences are Significant

workers or does not exist. Millennials were educated and prepared to start with zero and rapidly advance. Imagine how fast and far they would go if they started with the IK from your best and brightest older generation talent?

Work/Life balance has to do with flexibility of the time and location of work which has historically been dictated to specific times and locations in the Industrial Age workplace. There will be much more on this particular topic in later chapters.

It is time that work reflects Connected Age thinking. Connected Age thinking includes intentional empowered development, advancement, and work/life balance for all talent in the workplace.

Now that we have looked at work it is time to examine the two cultural "Age" shifts that initiated the approaching millennium change cycle (MCC) tsunami. We'll start with a quick overview summary in Chapter 6 of the two "Age" shifts. Then the next four chapters will more closely discuss the philosophic "Age" shift (Chapter 7) and elements of the business model "Age" shift – economics, technology, and pedagogy (Chapters 8, 9, & 10 respectively). As you'll see in these next five chapters, our current state of transformation validates more than ever the need to Unleash The Millennials and Save the World.

Unleash The Millennials and Save the World

Chapter 6

Cultural "Age" Shifts | Philosophic and Business Model

While doing research for Millennial leadership development in an organizational leadership doctoral program, I came across the idea of a not-so-normal generational clash in the workplace. I was reading numerous online articles having comments similar to the one that appeared in a 2013 Psychology Today article: "The Millennial generation… is transforming the nature of careers and the workplace. Their values, beliefs, and lifestyles are significantly different from the Baby Boomer generation. These differences will require organizations to adapt due to sheer numbers of Millennials who will dominate the workplace in the coming decade."[9]

The more I read the more I realized that something as significant as a cultural "Age" shift had occurred in the culture. Later I determined cultural age shifts had in-fact occurred through a philosophical Age collapse and a global transformation of business models from Industrial Age to Connected Age. The generational issues observed in the workplace between Boomers and Millennials was just a taste of the massive changes coming. The collapse of philosophical and business model Ages do not merely "pop up" but are reflective of deep cultural shifts infused in the minds of large groups of people and lived out in their behaviors.

In our immediate future, the changes, while large, are still manageable. As the millennium change cycle (MCC) tsunami continues to approach, and peaks post pandemic, every aspect of business will be affected, and the complexity of the change will become more difficult to handle. The implications of my research were significant enough that I started a coaching business aimed at helping organizations manage the immediate issues arising due to the coming changes.

The impending MCC tsunami will eventually result in something beyond anything any generation has imagined in possibly over 1000 years. This is not just gibberish to sell a book; look around and see the extreme upheavals in every area of society. There is a new normal as people become inured to the changes. We are in for a massive millennium change coming just in the next few years. My goal is to help companies survive the MCC tsunami crest, which will hit sometime around 2025, by Unleashing the Millennials and Saving the World.

I purposefully coined the term MCC tsunami to articulate the magnitude of the coming change and to let people know this is not a thunderstorm dumping a bit of rain, and maybe the electricity goes out, or even a hurricane, windy enough to blow down houses and trees. The MCC tsunami will be a total leveling of truth and knowability as well as the old business paradigm. This is an inundation! After the tsunami, the new and philosophically unchallenged Connected Age business model paradigm will emerge first from the receding water. How you make, sell, buy, bank, and the currency of exchange will all be different than it is even in 2020. The tsunami waters will not fully recede until the return of a philosophical age with theological underpinnings that reestablishes a foundation for truth and knowability. This will not occur for at least another generation or two.

The philosophical change happened in the West with the end of Modern Philosophy and subsequent collapse of 2600-years of the Age of Western Philosophy. The transformation from Industrial Age to Connected Age business models resulted primarily from major shifts in three foundational areas of culture, namely economics, technology, and pedagogy. These two cultural Age shifts (i.e. philosophical collapse and business model transformation) were essentially woven together and created the MCC Tsunami. About seventy-five percent of shifting in both areas was complete by the time the Millennial generation was being born in the early 1980s. The effects of the two Age shifts wiped out the U.S. adopted Industrial Age business model which began with the Industrial Revolution in England around 1740. Some vestiges of Industrial Age

Cultural "Age" Shifts | Philosophic and Business Model

businesses are still around, but upon closer examination you will see their roots are dead.

In the new environment, after the cultural Age shifts were fully underway and seventy-five percent complete, the ground was fertile and plowed open. The rise in technology during the 1970s through 1980s provided the seed. Fertilization of the seed occurred in the 1990s via the Internet. The Connected Age was born and began to grow below ground until it emerged into view between 2006 and 2010. The business model paradigm of the Connected Age will continue to evolve as it matures. The first part of that evolution is ongoing and includes Millennial talent.

When the MCC tsunami crests around 2025, the cultural age shifts will be complete, but their long-term impact will continue to unfold. The tsunami waters will level out as the last of the Boomers hit sixty-five by 2027. As the water begins to recede, Gen-Z workers will begin to enter the workforce and that's when the prolonged growth spurt into maturation will begin. As you read further about Millennials, double what Millennials have the potential to accomplish and you're still not close to the impact Gen-Z will have on the world.

You may think, "This is just speculation. It will never really happen." After you read the next four chapters, you may think a bit differently. In fact, I am very confident based upon everything I've read, and the patterns being revealed globally, that within ten years after the crest we will see a global millennium change happen as a direct result of something the Millennials initiate, and Gen-Z completes. The MCC tsunami precedes the change. It will either be catastrophic, or inspiring.

Between 2010 and 2014, writers and researchers began reporting on the effects of the cultural age shifts and the impact of Millennials in the workplace. These articles were related to Millennial views on work-life balance and education and technology differences among Millennials and older generations. Millennials were portrayed as disloyal to employers, comfortable walking away from jobs that they didn't want to do, or willing to take a similar job with a competitor making ten cents more an hour. At first, the sheer volume of these negative articles about Millennials made me think they were a broken generation. Digging deeper, I realized something more significant was going on. Millennials were not broken!

My curiosity was captured when reading about work-life balance among Millennials who viewed work as the "part of living" that provides an opportunity to be creative while making a wage sufficient for immediate needs. For them, work is not tied to a specific location and it needs to fit within a flexible schedule that allows them to participate in activities that fulfill them.

Boomers, on the other hand, had no balance. They had worked since they were wee-high and could cut grass, wait tables, baby sit, or wash cars. Life was what you did after work and before you went to sleep. Work occurred at a specific location involving repetitive tasks that produced sufficient results to keep you from getting fired or forcibly retired. Long hours and time away from family was assumed to just be part of the job if you wanted to get paid. Boomers all knew if you didn't work, you and your family didn't eat. Work, work, work. You can live after retirement.

The conflicts began when Boomers questioned Millennials' refusal to work long hours, or absence from their designated workstations during their working hours. The Millennials' response was typically that the Boomers "needed to get a life" and that their work could easily be done at home or a coffee shop with Wi-Fi after hours and certainly not at a specific desk or location. To the older generations, work was synonymous with long hours at a specific location, and for Millennials, work was synonymous with an untimed task. Location was irrelevant. Notice that everything is different. Also notice the pandemic required remote working demonstrates the Millennials were correct—admittedly depending upon the nature of the work. This was not a normal Industrial Age generational spat over the kids not picking up their toys.

The educational gap was due to specific changes in the educational process beginning in the early 1980s and continuing through the early 21st century. Up until the 1980s, education was an individual effort with students earning grades based upon their own work with only authorized assistance. The Millennials, however, were educated in groups increasingly connected as technology systems improved. The conflict came in when Millennials wanted to participate fully on Boomer teams, receiving all the key information, while Boomers wanted to keep their own work private. Again, totally different. And think about teamwork in your office today. The Millennials were right.

The final puzzle piece noted in the literature was technology. Boomers saw technology, accepted it, used it, loved it, and simultaneously hated it. On the other hand, the Millennials did not "see" technology at all. It was like oxygen: it was everywhere and 100% vital. The conflict came in when Boomers dreaded the next technology they had to learn while the Millennials embraced the change and, in fact, were the ones demanding the ever-increasing leaps made in technology. The Millennials were right.

The vastness of articles about Millennial lack of loyalty and entitlement in the workplace between 2010 and 2014 was extreme to the point of nausea. In short, Millennials are not disloyal or filled with a sense of entitlement. Rather they are the most educated, emotionally integrated, creative and innovative generation possibly in recorded history. The workspaces they were entering were not prepared for them; a new workspace needed to be created. I realized something totally new and awesome was coming that I didn't fully understand, so I looked deeper to find the reasons.

I picked the 2025 date as the crest of the MCC tsunami based on demographics, as demographic data is critical to the tsunami crest and the millennium change coming. By 2025, seventy-five percent of the global workforce will be Millennial. Xers will be the generation with the next largest workplace representation, followed by a small percentage of Gen-Z's just entering the workplace. Globally, Connected Age leaders will be in place in every aspect of society, not just business. Universities, medicine, government, military—everywhere. And, whatever humans do for work, there will be more Millennials than any other generation doing it. These Connected Age leaders will rapidly transform everything we understand as normal today into something we wouldn't recognize if we encountered now. The final step in the transformation into a lasting millennium change will happen within a generation or two following the MCC tsunami crest.

With all that as a background, let's jump into elements of the two cultural "Age" shifts—philosophy and business model paradigm (i.e. economics, technology, and pedagogy). Of the two shifts, the most expansive and impactful on Western culture is the collapse of Modern Philosophy and the end of 2600 years of Western Philosophy as we know it. The business model paradigm shift is obviously most influential in the workplace and affected by this philosophical collapse to one degree or another; significantly in many instances. This overview is not meant to be exhaustive, but just enough to provide you the background about what

Unleash The Millennials and Save the World

you're observing in the workplace and to convince you to Unleash The Millennials and Save the World.

Chapter 7

Philosophical Collapse | End of Modern Philosophy

A significant philosophical collapse occurred when Modern Philosophy ended in the 1950s and the Postmodern period filled the vacuum shortly thereafter. Postmodernism made its way from Europe to the U.S. in the early 1960s and was fully entrenched in the culture during the formative years of the Millennials. Let me restate that to give you an idea of the significance. This was only the third time a philosophy collapsed in 2600 years of Western Philosophy, and the Age of Western Philosophy as we know it ended with it. History shows that this is an enormously significant event that will have mindboggling consequences for decades to come. The reason few even realize it happened is that the collapse occurred in Europe, the seat of both the Modern Philosophy and of Western Philosophy as well. Boomers and many Xers in the U.S. were being born and raised and began working while the Postmodernism after-effect entered the U.S. culture. American Millennials were born after Postmodern thinking was fully entrenched.

We all think, because we haven't lived for a thousand years, that what we are experiencing is normal. A philosophic collapse is not normal. What Boomers lived through (i.e. the collapse of a Modern Philosophy), has only happened twice before. This particular collapse, in essence, ended a 2600-year domination of Western Philosophy in Western culture. While Eastern Philosophies (i.e. Asia – China, India, Japan) are still up and running, they are not a central focus of this book addressing the U.S. workplace. The economic engine of the world is dominated by the influence of Western Philosophy. In particular, the global economy was established under and is highly influenced by Modern Philosophy which was also instrumental in the development and expansion of the Industrial Age. The differences between Western and Eastern Philosophies are significant.

The standards for ethics, morality, and knowability in all three Western Philosophy Ages (Ancient, Medieval, and Modern) were transcendently seated in the writings and beliefs about the gods of the Greek and Roman pantheons, and the God of Judaism, Christianity, and Islam. What this means is that some transcendent entity or a mind outside, above, and superior to the realm of human existence established a bar(s) of conduct. Enforcement of conduct is locally applied temporally but ultimately each person is judged in the afterlife based upon what they have done.

I remember entering a new millennium (2000 CE) and all the fuss about ©Y2K. All computers were supposed to crash, planes fall out of the sky, industrial facilities explode, satellites become lost in space; you know, just another turning of the calendar type day. We were told to be prepared to wear a hard hat outside as you never knew what might be falling from the sky. Yet with my hard hat in hand and ready at any moment, nothing happened, likely as a result of all that went into making sure nothing happened.

We are all living in a time when Europe, the U.S., and all other Western countries do not have a common philosophical age with theological underpinnings that firmly establishes the ideals of truth and knowability. This isn't even talked about by the philosophers because over the past 150 years they've written themselves into a nihilistic corner with no escape plan. However, as opposed to Y2K, something did happen when Modern Philosophy collapsed, the consequences of which have only begun to be seen and which won't be settled until the next philosophical age is established.

The first Western Philosophy Age was Ancient Philosophy which lasted about 1100 years originating in Greece in the 6th century BCE and expanding into the Greco Roman world. The fall of the Western Roman Empire late in the 5th century CE precipitated the first philosophical collapse. The second Western Philosophy Age was Medieval Philosophy. It quickly arose after the collapse of Ancient Philosophy under the influence of Christian thought and lasted 1100 years from the 5th to 16th

century CE. The second philosophical collapse occurred in the 16th century shortly following the Reformation started when Martin Luther nailed his 95 theses to the church door.

Modern Philosophy filled the Medieval Philosophy void within Western Philosophy and was firmly entrenched for about 400 years from the 16th to 20th century CE. The third philosophical collapse and the end of Western Philosophy as we know it occurred in the mid-1950s shortly following WWII, with no philosophical age in view.

We are now living in a temporary philosophic holding period of "anti-philosophy" termed Postmodernism that filled the void made by the collapse of Modern Philosophy. It is, in essence, based upon artifacts of skepticism and cynicism that brought down the formerly well-ordered and recognized Modern Philosophy. Postmodernism is atheistic in origin and skeptical of any truth or knowability beyond what is considered true or knowable by individual social communities. While a philosophical collapse has occurred, it is unlikely that the anti-philosophy of skepticism and cynicism prevalent in Postmodernism will be the next philosophic age. Rather we are in a time of transition to a new philosophic age based upon propositional ideas about truth and knowability yet to be entered into philosophical discourse and debate. Remember, the philosophers still aren't talking about what happened. I'm assuming it is because of their skepticism.

Boomers were raised and educated in a Modern Philosophy culture (as were all previous U.S. generations), participated in the shift to a Postmodern culture, and have their feet planted firmly in both. Xers were raised and partially educated during the transition from a Modern to Postmodern philosophic culture and are predominantly Postmodern with some Modern philosophic artifacts. Millennials were raised in a totally Postmodern culture and are Postmodern in thought, word, and deed. We will examine what all this means. The implications to the workplace and culture at large are significant and widespread.

The entrance of Postmodern thought (founded upon atheism) into the U.S. began in the early 1960s and made huge inroads into the university systems, politics, and mainline denominational churches with strong European ties. It's rapid spread and acceptance by the masses can be easily understood when viewing the intellectual cultural undercurrent of philosophical atheism firmly established by the European philosophers of the 18th and 19th centuries. This philosophical atheism dominated the philosophy and theology departments of many if not the majority of this country's oldest and most prestigious colleges, universities, and seminaries by the mid-1950's in the U.S. Gone in Federal public discourse were the days when transcendent religious principles for ethics, morality, and knowability guided public decision-making. Instead, individual autonomy apart from any religious precepts was the guide moving forward.

Younger Xers and Millennials were raised in a Postmodern culture that was reinforced in everything they encountered, television programs, commercials, movies, literature, music, art, education, and architecture. The message was and still is that social constructs established up until the 1950s were the result of either outdated religious intolerance toward social ills or forced means of behavior by a ruling elite who had the means of enforcing behavioral standards through laws and the courts. This meant, culturally, that the history of the U.S. was something that must be purged and forgotten, by force if necessary, to ensure the U.S. never returned to a time when individual personal liberties were infringed upon by the majority for religious, political, and/or economic purposes.

It is the right of a Postmodern individual to do whatever her or she wants to do as long as it doesn't hurt or infringe upon the rights of anyone else. The cultural manifestation of Postmodern skepticism which we see currently is no different than the cultural manifestation of skepticism that was expressed in the Ancient Greco Roman world by Sophist rhetoricians in the 4th and 3rd centuries BCE. I think it important to look quickly at three such Sophist skeptics as ideas do repeat in history.

A Sophist named Gorgias used very influential rhetoric to introduce his radical skepticism that nothing was true or believable. He made the bold statement, "All statements are false." This could be compared with today's Postmodern maxim, "There are no absolute truths." Both statements are proven false by their own definitions, from which we can conclude that word "sense" is not important to the Skeptics. Rather, they hope to persuade people to believe whatever they tell them, truth or lie. At that point, Skeptics can do what they want to do and at the same time have you do what they want done.

Thrasymachus, another ancient Sophist Skeptic, thought that justice was not rooted in truth and nobility but in getting what a person wanted (i.e. "If I get what I want then that is justice for me."). In that light,

Philosophical Collapse | End of Modern Philosophy

Thrasymachus viewed the strongman who used his strength and whatever other resources available to forcibly get what he wanted was the man who acted in effectual justice. This "might makes right" form of justice was later adapted by Friedrich Nietzsche who posited that only the strong are worthy of surviving: his superman concept. Hitler was inspired by Nietzsche's writings and put those ideas into practice with catastrophic precision. Hitler and his henchmen believed they were doing the "just" thing. They were not crazy, but devout to their beliefs for establishing a superior Aryan race to rule the earth. Today, many fascist and nationalist movements, as well as the Antifa movement, are using such "might makes right" practices to enforce their disparate senses of justice.

Laws controlling society and the masses were viewed by Thrasymachus as the elite's way of limiting the power of the government so the governing elite could amass wealth through civil enslavement of citizens. This was a very similar argument used later by Karl Marx when he viewed that laws in place were for the benefit of the rich at the expense of the poor. Of course, we know that literally over 120 million people were murdered in the 20th century by revolutionary leaders whose implementation of Marx's ideology led to a "might makes right" reality. Listen to the rhetoric of extremists on both sides of the political spectrum and you'll see what they are espousing is not something new. Implementation of "corrective measures" demanded by rhetoricians has historically resulted in a killing field with streets filled with blood.

The third and most influential of our skeptical Sophists was Protagoras, who believed that humankind was the measure of all things. He is often thought as the first of ancient humanists. For Protagoras, all knowledge has its origin and ending in humankind alone. There is no such thing as objective truth (i.e. according to a standard outside of humans) but merely individual and culturally accepted truths. And while each person's knowledge and perceptions differ (appearance/perceptions and reality are the same things) then truth also differs person to person. What is true for one person can be false for another; in fact, it is to be expected. Both persons are correct. Of course, we see the exact same Protagoras thought today within the Postmodern framework of individual truth and no standard for absolute truth.

While Postmodern thought and related skepticism were enveloping every aspect of U.S. culture, technological development and scientific discovery kept marching along. We solved the genetic code (DNA), made dramatic steps in neuroscience ("what is the mind?"), discovered in subatomic physics the building block of matter—the Higgs boson, or the 'god particle'— and are well on our way to developing artificial intelligence (AI) that can process information faster than the human brain. Some say that AI will think on its own. With all these new discoveries there have been revivals of religious speculation about the existence of God or gods, a spiritual realm, and some form of mind-life after death, even among formerly staunch atheists.

Based upon the plethora of articles on the Internet, it is clear that many people believe the current political foment in the U.S. is aimed at totally dismantling Western culture. As noted earlier, this has been going on for over a century as proponents of 18th and 19th century philosophical atheism have been diligently working through the university systems, public education, and political arena to destroy all vestiges of Western Philosophy and its transcendent standards for ethics, morality, and knowability. Let me say that our Western Culture has always hinged upon transcendent truth and knowability being upheld by a Western Philosophy which we currently do not have.

Close at hand is a philosophic tipping point. The cultural understanding of individual human rights may flip to no understanding of human rights beyond what the ruling authority dictates. The only thing postponing this flip are the Boomers and Xers who still remember a time when transcendent principles were part of our cultural fabric. If the flip is allowed to occur unchecked, the U.S. will likely become another China; atheistic socialism with centralized control with just enough individual freedoms to allow economic growth. Sedition or rebellion at the federal and/or state level will quickly be addressed with exile or death of the radicals. It works and is working well in China. If you are wondering about this, just ask a citizen of Hong Kong who disagreed with China's recent policy to allow deportation into mainland China.

In the realm of business, we do not have decades to establish basic standards of behavior. The suggestion I make and support later in the book is to reestablish these standards at the workplace level. Adhering to standards is linked to who is the established authority (i.e. "Who says I have to behave this way?"). My suggestion is that there must be a truth and knowability of ethical and moral standards within every company or organization. If leadership establishes this standard, and expects it to be adhered to, it will establish right behavior. Do not look for any cultural norms in this Postmodern period to tell corporate talent not to lie, steal, cheat, or even murder. Ethical and moral standard establishment in terms of corporate truth and knowability is now required at the local level.

The sooner a standard is established with all generations in the workplace, the sooner the Millennials will pick up and observe the advantages of practicing true and knowable ethical and moral behavior patterns at work. Because work is inclusive of their life, they will also likely continue to practice the standards you establish in their time away from work. One company at a time we can together reestablish truth and knowability in the U.S. and reclaim some semblance of order out of disorder until a new philosophic age is established. Unleash The Millennials and Save the World.

Unleash The Millennials and Save the World

Chapter 8

Economic Shift | End of Industrial Age

An economic culture shift was underway in the U.S. during the time Boomers were being born (1946-1962) and was completed when Millennials were being born (1982-2000). The economic shift marked the end of U.S. dominance of Industrial Age production and manufacturing, i.e. making things. The economic shift reflected the beginning of an entirely new age, called the Connected Age which is discussed in the next chapter, in which the greatest economic growth and wealth creation was in the area of new knowledge emerging from data relationships and artificial intelligence. The economic shift had an impact on Boomers more than anyone else as they were born, raised, and educated to be active participants in the Industrial Age, which was becoming a mere memory. By the time the oldest Boomers reached their early forties, the economic shift was in full swing. Boomers still feels the impact with each passing year, made more difficult due to their inability to fully comprehend and actively engage in the new Connected Age business model economy.

The Industrial Age model dominated in the United States for well over 200 years. The Industrial Age began in Britain in the 1700s and is associated with a boom in science, mechanization, manufacturing, and automation. This was a time of great wealth creation and capitalism as productivity in the Western world shifted from hand-made to machine-made. Agriculture depended less and less on livestock and more on machines. Mass production became a reality. With a wealth of natural resources, available land, safe and bountiful ports of trade, and a growing

Unleash The Millennials and Save the World

population base, the U.S. soon began to lead the world in industrial and agricultural production.

Following the Civil War, the emphasis in the U.S. moved even more from agricultural production to industrial production. Pre-war industries expanded, and many new industries arose in rapid succession as new manufacturing and textile machinery were invented that utilized new sources of power (i.e. steam, electricity, internal combustion engines). Starting in the northeast and moving west and south was a whole new range of oil and gas refineries, electrical power plants, manufacturing facilities, steel foundries, and textile mills.

U.S. ports of national and international trade were soon booming, and inland waterways were used to move materials and products to and from production and population centers. Railroads along the east coast expanded west, moving people and creating opportunities for more expansion. Surface roads were constructed to allow greater ease of travel and trade within the footprint of the expansion and, in the 20th century, automobiles and trucks began to fill those roads. Electricity became available to the masses through the erection of transmission lines and power stations in remote areas, spawning further expansion.

This industrial production and manufacturing growth economically transformed U.S. society. It produced new classes of wealth previously not seen in our former agrarian economic system. We now had extremely wealthy industrialists, a new and expanding middle class, and a rapidly growing blue-collar working class. The need for labor in industrial and other rapidly expanding areas soon outstripped available labor sources even as many from rural areas flocked to the cities. This labor shortage attracted millions of immigrants from Europe and around the globe to permanently relocate and join our growing country. The wealth gap was still in place, but with a growing middle class benefitting from some of the wealth being produced.

The Industrial Age heyday in the U.S. lasted well over 150 years in earnest and made this once seemingly isolated and fledgling new country into the most prosperous economy on earth. Our industrial dominance began to wane in the late 1960s, and by the mid-1980s was essentially declining. There were many factors in the decrease in industrial manufacturing, which led to new industrial ages in other parts of the world.

Economic Shift | End of Industrial Age

The aftermath of WWII had a huge effect on the decline of the U.S. Industrial Age. During the war years, the U.S. stretched all its industrial resources to the very limits of production in almost every area. Relatively speaking, industries were using equipment that was neither new nor completely worn out at the start of the war. After the war, however, there was a plethora of industrial and manufacturing equipment and facilities that needed to be replaced or upgraded to new technologies. But money was tight and demands on industry still high, so reinvestment in the industrial and manufacturing complexes that had made us great were put off. Part of the production demands that held off reinvestment were the second cause of our decline as industrial giants in the world economy.

In wartime, one of the first duties of the military offensive is to take out the industrial production and manufacturing resources of the enemy. World War II was a very effective war in that regard as, over time, huge chunks of industry sectors, manufacturing, steel mills, refineries, chemical plants, electrical power plants, fuel storage, key roads, bridges, railroads, and electrical transmission facilities across Europe and Japan were badly damaged or destroyed. The U.S. had participated in the war but had been spared the ravages of war because of our distance from the fighting. Though our nation had already spent its industrial capacity during the war, we financed and supplied the industrial production and manufacturing for materials and technologies needed to rebuild what was destroyed in Europe and Japan during the war. And we didn't send them used stuff but rather the newest and latest technologies that we also badly needed but did not provide for ourselves.

By the mid to late 1950s, the industrial and manufacturing markets we used to dominate globally, even with worn out equipment and technologies, were being taken over by more efficient and cost-effective industrial production and manufacturing facilities we helped finance and build across Europe and Japan. In order to effectively compete with the new facilities and new technologies, we needed a long overdue retooling of our aging industrial and manufacturing complexes. However, economically, it was not entirely feasible in many sectors given the cost of investment versus the anticipated return from diminishing markets of opportunity now being dominated by foreign companies. However, new advances in chemical and petrochemical production did continue, allowing industrial expansion in those sectors in the Northeast and the

South. Unfortunately, the rest of our now global, commodity-priced, industrial production and manufacturing landscape in the U.S. began to go fallow.

The third contributing factor to the demise of the U.S. Industrial Age began in the 1960s and into the 1970s when public outcry against uncontrolled air, water, and waste pollution from industrial and manufacturing facilities and concern for the environment reached Washington D.C. In response, the federal government passed the Clean Air Act in 1963, the Clean Water Act in 1972, and the Resource Conservation and Recovery Act (RCRA) in 1976 (solid and hazardous waste disposal regulations). The cost of retrofitting existing industrial and manufacturing facilities to meet the new standards was huge and, in some cases, cost prohibitive.

Those companies whose core businesses were impacted by these new regulations and who faced costly retrofitting to meet the standards in existing facilities began to look for opportunities outside of the United States to build new facilities that did not have to meet the new U.S. pollution control regulations. What they discovered were very cooperative foreign governments desiring the investment and offers of cheap labor compared to the wages paid for similar work in the U.S. It was a double win for U.S. companies if favorable trade agreements were in place to allow ease and low cost of entry of their products back into their primary market. By the early 1980s it became evident that new major greenfield type industrial and manufacturing investment and development in the U.S. was over and had moved initially to Mexico, then to Asian countries, and finally to the behemoth of population and future markets, China—now the world's second largest economy and climbing.

While environmental concerns were one of the nails in the coffin for the Industrial Age, it was a nail worth driving home. I can remember in the mid-1960s the haze of pollution over my hometown and the strong smell of hydrocarbons in the air from the refinery and chemical plants in our area. A clear day was unusual and generally meant a cold front had blown through. And I can also remember that by the early 1980s we had blue-sky days, no unpleasant smell in the air, and truck drivers weren't dying from deadly fumes from the loads of chemicals they emptied into unrestricted disposal pits. Recent travels to China reminded me of those days. The unbelievable air pollution there was once our "normal" in the

Economic Shift | End of Industrial Age

U.S. I was glad to breathe clean air and drink clean water from the tap when I got home. Other benefits to the regulations were widespread and included getting many endangered species off the list, a decline in rates of cancer and other diseases, and a reduction in birth defects.

The fourth and a relatively newly acknowledged and major component in our economic shift were trade deficits caused by currency manipulation by our major trading partners. When large trading partners artificially reduce the value of their currency against the U.S. dollar, their products become much cheaper than those same products made in the U.S. This artificial manipulation lowers the cost of U.S. imports and raises the cost of U.S. exports. Ending the practice of artificial currency manipulation can significantly push back upon the economic shift and allow positive growth in industrial production and manufacturing to return to the U.S. It should be noted that while healthy industrial production and manufacturing would be welcome, the Industrial Age in the U.S. is dead.

The globalization of industrial production and manufacturing has created a new planet-wide economy of trade on a major scale. Just look at the tag on any product you buy. Where was it made? Check the instruction guide or user manual for a product and see how many languages are used. There was a time not so long ago (say late 1960s to mid-1970s) when virtually everything you purchased in a store was made start to finish from industrial products and manufacturing facilities located in the U.S. Foreign manufactured imports were extremely unusual and often viewed as inferior to similar products made in America. As foreign competition entered our markets, at first with inferior but cheap products, our own manufacturers had to meet or beat the price. Product quality declined as U.S. manufacturers tried to make things more cheaply and soon it made more sense to buy the foreign products. Dollar to dollar, they became the preferred purchase.

Validation of this economic shift is found in terms of the trade balance of imports and exports. More than three-fourths of all traded goods in the U.S. are manufactured products. Exports boost U.S. output production and imports reduce U.S. output production. The more we export, the more demand there is for U.S. manufactured products. The more we import, the demand for manufactured goods goes down. The U.S. has netted a trade deficit every year since 1974 (i.e. importing more than exporting).[10] Efforts are currently being made to create a resurgence in

Unleash The Millennials and Save the World

U.S. industrial production and manufacturing in an attempt to rebalance our trade deficit and keep more U.S. dollars here than we send abroad on imports.

Millennials born in the 1980s and beyond were not raised, educated, and trained to work in the Industrial Age economy of making things. They were raised, educated, and trained to work in the new Connected Age business economy of technology—a completely different mindset than Industrial Age thinking. The turnaround in creativity and innovation in Industrial Age enterprises will occur as Millennials are provided answers for the "Why and How" questions and are developed, advanced, and provided work/life balance in thier assignments. I'm confident that in the new global economy of industrial production and manufacturing, the innovation of our Millennials will begin to revive a superior standard of quality in our manufactured products at a globally competitive price. But no matter the result, the reality is the same. The Industrial Age in the U.S. is over.

In the next chapter we'll explore the evolution of technology which happened very quickly, ultimately getting us to the present—the Connected Age. The Industrial Age lasted well over 300 years and we are still in the infancy of this new era. What is possible in this Connected Age is staggering in scope. After the millennium change in a generation or two, those possibilities are beyond imagination. The generation that will witness both the millennium change and the unfolding of incomprehensible Connected Age transformation is here now. Unleash The Millennials and Save the World.

Chapter 9

Technologic Shift | Beginning of Connected Age

A major cultural shift in the United States happened because of massive advances in technology. The rise of a new technology-based age began in earnest in the early 1960s with advances in computer technology and the subsequent networking of computers (computers talking to computers). One particularly profound shift happened when military command and control communications could be connected through a packet switching system as a means of staying securely connected in case of nuclear attack. This change made it possible to avoid communication breakdown and critical information loss in the event of a command center being destroyed, because the vital information was now everywhere on a network not just in one location. Some say that this particular technological advance was revolutionary on the same order of magnitude as the printing press.[11]

This packet switching system concept was developed in 1962 by RAND Corporation and put into place in 1969 through funding by the Advanced Research Projects Agency (ARPA).[12] Later called the ARPANET, the military application was stripped in 1983 and the remaining network turned over to the public sector and used initially at the university level. Voila! The Internet was born. By the mid-90s, computer-based technological advances in the workplace using the Internet created a new global age of connectivity, replication, and commerce.

Unleash The Millennials and Save the World

Envisioning the coming changes that technology was bringing to the workplace, Peter Drucker, in his 1969 book The Age of Discontinuity, coined the term "knowledge worker." Drucker argued that knowledge workers were soon going to be the predominant employees within new industries as opposed to manual workers.[13] As computer technology advanced and the interconnection of the Internet expanded rapidly, Drucker's argument became a reality. Machines were now doing jobs once done by human hands. The humans behind those machines never put their hands on the process or products that resulted from their knowledge work.

When it was apparent by the end of the 1970s that the Industrial Age was ending, a quest was undertaken to name what was coming next. The first name given to this new age was the Technology Age. This name lasted from the early 1980s to mid-1990s and reflected the rapid rise and proliferation in the workplace environment of desktop computers, laptops, and digital devices of many kinds.

With the connection of public, private, and business sectors on the Internet in the early 1990s and the vast informational resources now available with a few clicks, a new name took precedence—the Information Age. Soon the entry cost of desktop computing sufficiently dropped, allowing Internet connected devices into classrooms at all levels across the country. The availability of electronic resource information in schools began to have a direct impact on education and learning as we will see in the next chapter. However, the Information Age name appeared short-lived, because in the late 1990s, hyper-speculation about and investment in something termed e-commerce captured the collective imagination. There were many who believed business and electronic currency-based transactions would soon be possible on an Internet-based platform.

Following a rather major hiccup in Internet-based stocks in 2000, the companies with vision and staying power emerged from the crash with a force, vigor, and immediate influence previously unseen in the world. The Internet allowed the unique combining of diverse technologies and disparate information to be connected and assimilated, and what's called the Connected Age came into existence. The Technology Age was a time where knowledge was converted into electronic signals, stored, and utilized. The Information Age was a time when silos of knowledge were

Technologic Shift | Beginning of Connected Age

able to be shared on the Internet. The Connected Age is the time when all knowledge is connected, seemingly without limit (e.g. the Internet of things).

To give you an idea of how significant this shift in technology has been and the economics behind it, the top six global companies by market value are all integral to participation in the Connected Age. Presented below are these six companies, their market value as of the first quarter of 2020, and the year they were founded. Note, no Industrial Age company is at the top, nor will they be in the future; the Age has changed.

Market Capitalization of Publicaly Traded Companies 1st Quarter 2020		
Company	Value ($B)	Yr. Founded
Microsoft	1200	1975
Apple	1100	1976
Amazon	971	1994
Alphabet	799	1998
Alibaba	522	1999
Facebook	475	2004

Source: https://en.wikipedia.org/wiki/List_of_public_corporations_by_capitalization#2020
Last accessed April 19, 2020

This shift from the Industrial Age to the Connected Age directly affected the expansion of human knowledge. This expansion was calculated and called the "knowledge doubling curve" by Buckminster Fuller who showed that until 1900, human knowledge doubled approximately every 100 years.[14] This doubling increased to every twenty-five years after WWII. David Schilling estimated that, in 2013, human knowledge expansion was doubling every twelve months. According to Schilling, "…the build out of the 'internet of things' will lead to the doubling of knowledge every 12 hours."[15] The next advent of the

Connected Age will be the roll-out of artificial intelligence (AI) that will harness new knowledge formulation.

Boomers and older Xers raised, educated, and trained in the Industrial Age found themselves in an entirely new Connected Age, but they didn't transition their work style. They didn't and still don't fully comprehend the implications of the fact that the Industrial Age workstyle is no longer relevant! As a Boomer, I can say that it hurts to write that truth. It's time Boomers and older Xers made themselves relevant in their last few years of productivity in the Connected Age. If you don't believe me, read on…

The shift from the Industrial to the Connected Age also affected the understanding of what constitutes a full day's work. Alex Durand writes,

> The key difference between the two is that in an economy of goods, workers performed rote mechanical tasks and could optimally do so for eight hours a day… the [economy of services] knowledge worker has the capacity for six hard mental work hours per day. Beyond hour six, you can no longer expect optimal productivity from your knowledge worker.[16]

This is a critical element when thinking of work-life balance issues and could provide a strategic advantage for any company figuring out where that balance rests. Specifically, after what number of hours of high production, using a digital device, do additional hours start providing diminishing returns?[17]

The Millennials have known nothing but the Connected Age growing up, through their education and life experience. While now living in the Connected Age, the minds of Boomers and, to a lesser extent, Xers are still drawing from Industrial Age paradigms. Think of the paper and pen and face to face handshake paradigm versus one based on global video conferencing, georeferenced 3D imagery, and electronic currency exchange, and you'll see the disconnect.

And here's the huge kicker. Boomers rarely articulate their utter frustration with the Connected Age and the pace of technological advancement outside of a very close and trusted professional peer group. There is great fear among this aging group of workers that if others knew how lost they feel in today's Connected Age, they would be replaced. They

Technologic Shift | Beginning of Connected Age

think that keeping quiet and holding on to key institutional knowledge will keep them safe until retirement. This is not a smart path forward for anyone, employee, manager, or business.

Millennials are fully committed Connected Age citizens and entirely capable of taking over many industry sectors now. They don't think they need the Boomer institutional knowledge (IK), and they really don't. But having that institutional knowledge would give them a huge leg up on their global competition, something we'll look at in a later chapter. Provide Millennials the "Why and How" answers around your IK and watch creativity and innovation soar. Allow them development opportunities, advance them rapidly in accordance with their competency, and allow them to exercise work/life balance in whatever they pursue.

What we have an opportunity to accomplish in the near and long term is monumental. We are not just doing Industrial Age trade with neighboring communities and states but Connected Age business with every part of the world. The difference between a potential U.S. market population of 350+ million (which is pretty big) is really not even in the same universe of comparison with a potential global market population of 7+ billion, all of it just one click away. It is time for Boomers to get your Millennial talent out of your Industrial Age business model. Your making-things paradigm must intentionally shift to the Connected Age paradigm of doing things with technology. Hurry! Before it is too late for you or your company to survive over the next five years.

Success in Western culture throughout history has always hinged upon the education of the next generation. In the next chapter, we'll examine changes in pedagogy (teaching methods and rubrics) that were necessary to prepare students for future career paths vastly different than anything ever encountered in the history of the world. They have been specifically prepared to address what is ahead. Unleash The Millennials and Save the World.

Unleash The Millennials and Save the World

Chapter 10

Pedagogic Shift | Educating Connected Age Workforce

With significant shifts in philosophy, economics, and technology occurring in the culture and workplace environment, educational pedagogy at all levels, from pre-K through graduate school, began to be rethought and retooled in the mid-1980s. The question addressed was, "What is needed to address educational requirements for a new workplace environment in light of technological advances?" How would changing metrics, measurements, methods, and means in education translate into preparing graduates for a workplace environment not yet fully defined. The education needed to work in the Industrial Age was relatively straightforward and addressed needs ranging from manual and skilled labor, management, and planning, to executive leadership and finance. The pedagogy for students to meet the needs of the Industrial Age had been honed over several hundred years around the globe. But what was needed to prepare the knowledge workers whom Drucker had identified years earlier?

In order to produce knowledge workers, pedagogy changed to address the envisioned challenges students would face upon graduating and entering the workforce. Jane Bluestein presented an extensive comparison of the traditional classroom where Industrial Age workers learned to today's classroom that is preparing students for the Connected Age. Bluestein noted the differences between the two classrooms are stark and include areas such as, "classroom values, priorities, motivators, authority relationships, desired (encouraged) student behaviors, and discipline goals."[18] Connected Age Millennials have been taught to think, behave, and create much differently than their Industrial Age employers and supervisors. But it has not stopped there.

The Connected Age business model economy was a relatively new idea in 2006 and was pointing to a new reality. Anne Zelenka, in a 2007 blog article on GIGAOM, noted that the transition from the Information Age to the Connected Age also included a shift in worker designation from knowledge worker to web worker.[19] Zelenka distinguished the two as follows: "Knowledge workers create and manage information, massaging it into intangible knowledge goods. Web workers create and manage relationships across knowledge goods, hardware, and people."[20]

To paint the short-lived Information Age with a broad brush—it was associated with a top down accessing of information from disparate sources (silos) for assimilation and use with licensed products. The Connected Age, using a similar broad brush, is associated with open and transparent connection and collection of the disparate information silos into single large data sets termed metadata. The huge metadata mountain is then mined to assimilate and synthesize relationships creating entirely new knowledge from the information.

The realization of the implications of the Connected Age economy on the educational system was most dramatically articulated in a 2011 book by Cathy N. Davidson of Duke University in which she wrote, "Fully sixty-five percent of today's grade-school kids may end up doing work that hasn't been invented yet."[21] Schools began sifting through the possibilities, acquiring new technology, and implementing new programs to develop proper pedagogy for those Connected Age jobs most likely on the near term horizons, though how could they know what jobs they were actually preparing students for? Thus began a quest to develop pedagogy for jobs not yet invented.

The educational shift in secondary schools, colleges and universities away from Industrial Age workers to Connected Age workers has had a significant impact on Millennials graduating from college and trying to enter a predominantly Industrial Age-managed workforce. Students were being educated for future job possibilities not of Industrial Age origin but for existing jobs and possibilities in Connected Age companies. Taught in an environment where (ideally) students are on an even sociological footing, the predominant shift is away from individual work to

Pedagogic Shift | Educating Connected Age Workforce

accomplish specific known tasks (Industrial Age mindset) to open and transparent group work to play with possibilities and discovery (Connected Age mindset).

Industrial Age education for Boomers was siloed into subject matter (i.e. reading, writing, arithmetic, science, etc.) and done in rows and columns of desks in a classroom with a teacher as the expert. Lectures were given, homework assigned, and students were responsible for their own work. Student learning was individualized and measured through testing and written assignments with an objective grading rubric. The Industrial Age education model produced students who were individually goal-focused, outcome-oriented, and task-based. This means that tasks were to be systematically completed to produce desired outcomes that would eventually result in goal achievement.

In Industrial Age education students did their own work on assignments except in rare instances of group work when given specific instructions and explicit permission by the teacher. In instances where group study was allowed, students were held to an honor system that did not allow them to give answers to fellow students or to share work of any kind. In this environment, Boomers learned to hide their work and be suspicious of anyone who tried to copy or get their individualized information. If a teacher caught a Boomer student doing otherwise (i.e. voluntarily allowing their individualized information to be seen by another), the student would be given a zero for the assignment and probably be sent to the principal for a few swats from the paddle to reinforce the lesson.

Industrial Age education was meant to prepare a workforce for immediate success in both trade crafts and college. Entrance to college was selective for the most prestigious colleges and universities but for most local colleges and state universities minimal entrance requirements needed to be met. White Americans who wanted to go to college and had decent grades and the money to pay reasonable tuitions could do so. Once in college, the need to excel academically was a personal preference and not a matter of intense competition. You did what you had to do to graduate and get a job.

Connected Age education evolved away from Industrial Age learning in every way. Rather than siloed individual learning, students in Connected Age classrooms are taught in groups and learn subjects in relation to one

Unleash The Millennials and Save the World

another. Making connections among disciplines is valued and encouraged. STEM is an acronym for the combining of science, technology, engineering, and math. Some educators and schools include the arts in that combination and the acronym becomes STEAM. While individual subjects may still be taught, the teacher in the classroom is charged with helping the students make connections among the ideas and materials. The teacher is no longer expected to be only an expert in subject matter but also to act as a facilitator of student learning. Ideas, not just facts, are valued. Teachers introduce the subject matter and identify the best resources in the field of information on the subject, from hardcopy and Internet sources. Student teams are then given an assignment to complete and the fun begins as students investigate, communicate, cooperate, collaborate, and co-create (C4) assignment solutions. There may be more than one way to get to multiple answers and multiple solutions depending upon the application.

The students learn inductively through applied research and application of principles rather than deductively from being told what to do. They work together on assignments using whatever resources are available, with input and guidance from the teacher. Individual work, while important, is not given as much value as it once was. Collaborative and co-creative learning is emphasized and more valued than it was when Boomers were in school. This learning is done within an environment where it is known that individualized standardized testing will likely determine an individual's advancement in grade level and college acceptance. This individual autonomy for subject matter accountability does not hinder the classroom group and team-oriented work. Rather it reinforces the need for each individual member of the group or team to master the subject matter and not simply ride the coattails of others in the team.

Connected Age pedagogy produces students who are discovery-focused, mastery-oriented, and play-based. Millennials have been taught that a playful, connected approach (i.e. group and independent research, discussing findings with others, learning what others think, etc.) develops mastery. As mastery of the subject is achieved, entirely new discoveries occur as they relate what they've learned to a broad spectrum of subjects (STEM or STEAM). Millennials are not silo subject-minded but have a broad appreciation of the power of knowledge in multiple fields. And best of all, they are empowered to think independently and trust their own minds.

Connected Age pedagogy was not designed or implemented to prepare students for traditional trade crafts such as welding, plumbing, auto repair, electronics repair, etc. (and we are paying a big price for that now), but to prepare them for college and knowledge work. The Millennial generation is huge, and more of them went to college than generations past. With this percentage increase in the number of high school graduates who continued to college, colleges and universities across the country raised their entrance standards and, of course, their cost.

In addition, as the rest of the world was industrializing, it began sending their best and brightest to be educated in U.S. colleges and universities. The number of available seats shrank. Increased entrance standards and intense competition for available slots put pressure on U.S. students to increase performance not just in academics and standardized entrance examinations (i.e. ACT and SAT) but in extra-curricular activities as well. This trifecta of college entrance pressure (academics, standardized testing, extra-curricular activity) produced the most educated high school graduates and well-rounded generation in U.S. history (i.e. Millennials). And the Gen-Z students (born after 2002) that follow are Millennials-on-steroids.

Once into college, tremendous academic pressure continued for Millennials as the intellectual caliber of students in the classrooms was at an all-time high and showing no signs of decline. The education received by Millennials as a whole is nothing short of spectacular compared to the college education received by the majority of their Boomer supervisors. What Millennials lack in experience they far make up for in preparation for Connected Age work.

The problem for Millennial graduates is that the group and play mentality they've been educated within since pre-K does not assimilate well in predominantly Industrial Age professions and company environments that are still subject matter and individualized task based. One of the biggest struggles in Industrial Age businesses today is a lack of innovation. Is there any question now why that is happening?

Let me ask my Boomer readers, have you ever wondered why the newest Millennial hire just walks into your office and asks what you're working on? And while you're still thinking how to respond or in the

Unleash The Millennials and Save the World

process of saying "none of your business," they walk behind your desk and start looking at your computer screen and the piles of papers on your desk. Then as you are trying to confront them about being out of line, they ask, "Why are you working on that?" At this point you are extremely frustrated with Millennials in general and their "sense of entitlement," thinking they have any right to know what you are working on and why. Remember, you were educated (and maybe indoctrinated with swats) not to voluntarily share your work. And the Millennial who entered your office is now wondering what you're trying to hide by not sharing. You are seen as uncooperative, while you view the Millennial as out of line.

When the miffed Millennial finally leaves your office, neither of you wants anything to do with the other. At this point you can't wait for retirement and to take your institutional knowledge with you. And at the same time, the Millennials can't wait for the old geezer (that's you) to retire and get out of their way. Neither of you understands the value of the institutional knowledge you have, and how much more meaningful it could be were it innovated.

There are only a few years left to resolve this pedagogical disconnect and through communication, cooperation, collaboration, and co-creation (C4) to creatively innovate upon current company owned institutional knowledge (IK) which otherwise will never be fully revealed by Boomers. As was noted earlier, the Boomers are afraid of being displaced by younger and less expensive Connected Age talent and so they hold onto IK as their anchor in the chair— "If I give a Millennial my IK anchor, I will be floated out the door." What they do not realize is that Millennials don't want their chair. To them, that chair represents long boring Boomer days, and a nose to the grindstone. What Millennials want is to learn what Boomers know and think about the business and what it is doing and then C4 with the Boomer a way to take it to the next level.

In my research, I found a great comparison between the expectations of Industrial Age and Connected Age workers, presented in the following table. Based upon the descriptions provided in the table, it is clear that challenges in the workplace due to generational differences exist.

Workplace Expectations	
Industrial Age	**Connected Age**
Command and control management	Active, involved leadership
Individually focused work	Collaborative teamwork
Managed flow of information	Unstructured flow of information
Job security	Employability
Work = income	Work = Income & personal enrichment
Structure	No structure, flexibility is highly valued
Inward looking	Outward looking
Influence thru organizational position	Influence thru networks/communities

Source: Jessica Brack, Maximizing Millennials in the Workplace, (Chapel Hill, NC: UNC Kenan-Flagler Business School, 2012), 6, accessed March 7, 2015, http://www.kenanflagler.unc.edu/ executive-development/custom-programs/~/media/DF1C11C056874DDA8097271A1ED48662.ashx.

The President of Bentley University in Boston, one of the nation's leading business universities, noted that they funded a study in 2013 to "...gain an understanding of how key stakeholders define career preparedness; how they rate Millennial preparedness; and, what they believe can be done to ensure that Millennials graduate from college ready for success in the workplace."[22] Part of the Bentley study included having various groups giving a letter grade, A to F, for how universities prepared Millennials for the workplace. The following groups gave universities a "C" or below for preparing Millennials for the workplace: 61 percent of business decision-makers; 63 percent of parents; and 66 percent of the college graduates.[23] In addition, the study found that sixty-eight percent of recruiters say it is difficult for their companies to manage Millennials. When the survey asked recent college graduates who is to blame for their level of preparedness, 60 percent of the respondents blamed themselves.[24]

What these Millennials were encountering when entering the workforce were Industrial Age workplace environments. Management was top down; culture was do as you are told; workspaces were for working; and communication, cooperation, collaboration, and co-creation (C4) were for those with earned privileges. Millennials have been educated their entire lives for a completely different workplace environment. Management is a group effort; culture is organic and inclusive; workspaces are open and encourage play; and communication, cooperation, collaboration, and co-creation (C4) are universal. Progress is being made in this area and I'm hoping this book will give those who have yet to reinvent their workplace into a Connected Age environment a reason to start.

The ultimate goal is to have Millennials fluent in the "Why and How" things are done and provided opportunities for development, advancement, and work/life balance. This seemingly simple strategy will absolutely provide transitional Millennials within your organization who will create for you a stellar Connected Age workplace. When you finish this book you'll be ready to start now!

With all that has been written herein as an introduction, let's finally meet the Millennials. Let's see who they are and how they think. And most importantly, why they are the KEY to reestablishment of truth and knowability and business survival in the next few years as the millennium change cycle (MCC) tsunami crests. Also, we'll examine how they and Gen-Z are integral in the next two generations to ensure the coming millennium change results in our survival and not destruction. Without question or hesitation: Unleash The Millennials and Save the World!

Chapter 11

Who Are Millennials? | Welcome to Connected Age

The information in this section about the characteristics and formative influences on the Millennial generation comes primarily from large and small public and private surveys and related journal and magazine articles read while doing research on Millennials between 2010 and 2019. A U.S. Chamber of Commerce Foundation research-based report published in 2012 on the Millennial generation opens with this comment: "Millennials are likely the most studied generation to date. According to U.S. Census Bureau statistics, there are plenty of them to study, 80 million plus (the largest cohort size in history)."[25]

I've included multiple text citations in this chapter to emphasize the point that our cultural understanding of Millennials shifted dramatically after 2010 and, beginning in 2017, observations have been very positive. Yet the early, negative perceptions of Millennials that were in the literature through 2010 linger in the minds of many Boomers. Perception is reality. I think it is important to review and dispel outdated perceptions my readers may still have about possibly the greatest generation in human history—Millennials.

As you read the cited literature in this chapter, keep the above timeline in mind. The earlier, less than complimentary, articles were not being written by Millennials. After 2010, Millennials began answering their critics. Also recognize that the non-Millennials writing the earlier articles were viewing Millennials, who had been perfectly prepared to enter a Connected Age workplace, from an Industrial Age mindset.

Unleash The Millennials and Save the World

The earliest writing I encountered in my research into Millennials was an article by Brian O'Reilly, published in the July 24, 2000 issue of Fortune, entitled, "Meet The Future: It's Your Kids."[26] The piece presents the results of interviews and focus groups conducted with more than 220 mostly high school students in nine states and twelve cities. The survey was the combined effort of Fortune, Youth Intelligence (a youth marketing company), and Towers Perrin (a large human resource issue consultant). O'Reilly reports, "We asked about their career plans, social concerns, and anxieties; about their attitudes toward money, their relationships with friends and family, and their expectations for the future."[27] The description of the survey findings starts with the following:

> In the beginning, the process felt clumsy and about as scientific as reading tea leaves. The kids love money. They disdain money. They want challenging careers. They want a grass hut on a desert island. The kids at Rumson-Fair Haven High in New Jersey hijacked the conversation and kept talking about parenting and family life when there were more important topics to get to. The dots weren't connecting. But ever so slowly, as researchers came back and compared notes, a surprisingly consistent picture began to form, like that LIFE magazine cover where all the tiny photographs really do create an image of Marilyn Monroe when viewed from afar.[28]

The picture presented in the 2000 Fortune article reflected that Millennials were warm, confident, upbeat, and optimistic about finding good jobs apart from entitlement. They wanted to be well-educated and were willing to work hard. On the flip side, O'Brien notes, "...they are under severe stress, often from Boomer parents desperate to raise trophy kids with perfect grades, drop-dead résumés, and early admission to Harvard."[29] O'Brien saw a disconnect between the seemingly crushing pressure Millennials were under to get a great education and their aspirations after college. He noted, "They show scant interest in climbing ladders... disdain office cubicles... see no prestige in corner offices... [are not] impressed by what inspires Gen Xers.... [M]ost seem turned off by

Who Are Millennials? | Welcome to Connected Age

the obsessiveness and hideous hours required of Silicon Valley millionaires."[30]

The conclusions of the Fortunes article's primary author O'Reilly are reflected in his comments, quoted below. They reveal an outward lampooning of Millennial efforts to improve upon what the Boomer generation had already accomplished. He also reveals the often-cloaked hope of the Boomers that the Millennials would finally fix what was wrong with the world. This is an example of what makes an editorial piece so powerful culturally at changing the way people think:

> It's impossible to predict how and where the Millennials will apply their down-to-earth talents and inclinations. Maybe they'll plug the Internet into every refrigerator and lawn mower in the land. Master the human genome and live to be 200. Perfect electric cars. Even invent a good light beer. On the other hand, maybe they'll figure out how to do what the Boomers and Xers failed at so miserably: Simplify life. Balance work and family. Divide child rearing equitably between husband and wife. Give kids an education without giving them an ulcer. Reinvent middle-class life in America.[31]

The findings presented in the Fortune article were similar to those presented in a book by Neil Howe, published shortly after the article, in September 2000, and entitled, Millennials Rising: The Next Great Generation.[32] Similar to O'Reilly, Howe saw a great potential future for Millennials, noting, "Only a few years from now, this can-do youth revolution will overwhelm the cynics and pessimists. Over the next decade the Millennial generation will entirely recast the image of youth from downbeat and alienated to upbeat and engaged—with potentially seismic consequences for America."[33] Sounds like he knew about the millennium change cycle (MCC) tsunami before I did!

The Fortune article previously mentioned is important because it reflects what is found in the literature. Boomers and Xers controlled the initial flow of information, observations, and institutional studies on the Millennial generation and appeared biased toward the view that somehow the new generation entering the workforce (i.e. Millennial) was broken. The economic standard used in the articles and studies for determining workforce preparation was an Industrial Age one.

The intensive study of the Millennial generation began in earnest between 2000 and 2006. Literally hundreds and possibly thousands of articles can be found in mainstream newspapers and magazines as well as research-based journal articles by academic faculty, department heads, researchers, and administrators. The earliest articles found in my literature review typically described the changing demographic of the student population on college campuses across the country and the possible impact of these Millennial collegians when they enter the workforce.[34]

While many of these articles were interesting to read, I found very little written about the characteristics of Millennials in regard to work until about 2007. In 2006, Pew Research Center, in association with PBS, conducted an extensive survey and research project for a 2007 documentary series entitled, Generation Next.[35] The initial findings, published in 2007, were expanded on in a 2010 survey and a subsequent Pew Research report that included a side-by-side comparison of Millennial generation responses with those of older generations.[36] This 2010 Pew Research Center report was significant in that a large percentage of the magazine and journal articles that appeared in print following the report used the findings of these two Pew studies as their foundational research.

In the broadest sense, the earlier literature (prior to 2010) characterized Millennials as overwhelmed, over-connected, over-protected, and over-served.[37] They were observed to be paradoxical both generationally and individually. Articles and studies between 2012 and 2014 began reflecting that the Millennial generation was not broken but merely a reflection of normal generational evolution in the Connected Age. Millennials themselves had written and conducted many of these studies and articles that reflected a Connected Age mindset.

As the earliest Millennials entered the workforce, demographers were fearful that that generation would never grow up because they were unable to. One author noted: "They [demographers] fear that whatever social machinery was used in the past to turn kids into adults has now broken down, that society no longer provides young people with the moral backbone and the financial wherewithal to take their rightful place in the adult world."[38] I think this was an inkling the demographers had of the philosophical collapse and loss of transcendent truth and knowability in regard to morals and ethics, having everything to do with modern culture and nothing to do with Millennials specifically.

More positive articles began to appear after 2010 when the results of statistically valid surveys from extensive studies on Millennial characteristics at work began to be published. One highly significant survey was the subject of an article co-authored by Jeanne Meister and Karie Willyerd that appeared in the Harvard Business Review. Entitled "Mentoring Millennials," this article includes a table based on the polling of 2,200 professionals across a broad swath of industry. It provides a clear understanding of what Millennials are searching for in their work.

Presented below are things noted in the Harvard Business Review article that Millennials want from their boss and company, and to learn for their particular career paths through training, mentoring, and coaching.[39] These do not seem to be unreasonable expectations and are, in fact, the same things desired by Xers and Boomers.

Top Five Characteristics Millennials Want		
...from their boss	...from their company	...to learn
Will help me navigate my career path	Will help develop my skills for the future	Technical skill in my area of expertise
Will give me straight feedback	Has strong values	Self-management and personal productivity
Will mentor me and coach me	Offers customizable options in benefits/rewards package	Leadership
Will sponsor me for formal development programs	Allows me to blend work with the rest of my life	Industry or functional knowledge
If comfortable with flexible work schedules	Offers a clear career path	Creativity and innovation strategies

Source: Jeanne Meister and Karie Willyerd, "Mentoring Millennials," Harvard Business Review, May 2010, accessed October 1, 2014, http://hbr.org/2010/or/mentoring-Millennials/.

Beginning in 2011, and continuing for several years, The University of North Carolina (UNC) Kenan-Flagler Business School presented several executive training classes specifically aimed at helping business leaders negotiate the realities of Millennials entering corporate America. In the introduction of her materials, Jessica Brack writes,

Unleash The Millennials and Save the World

> They [Millennials] view the world differently and have redefined the meaning of success, personally and professionally. In some cases, this has led to misunderstanding among the generations co-existing in today's workplace. Increasingly, however, business leaders are realizing this generation's unique competencies and perspectives, and employers are looking for a way to harness their strengths.[40]

The extent of the generational gap in the workplace was most prominent in a large population survey of over 6,300 job seekers and human resource (HR) professionals. Conducted in 2013, the survey illustrates how Millennials described themselves and how HR professionals described Millennials in the workplace. In particular, three areas of extreme differentiation included:

2013 Survey of Millennials and HR Professionals Rating Perceived Character Qualities of Millennials		
Character Quality	Millennials	HR Professionals
People-Savvy	65%	14%
Hardworking	86%	11%
Loyal to Employer	82%	1%

Source: Beyond.com, "The Great Divide, Workplace Perceptions That Millennials Need to Rise Above." Visually, May 28, 2013. Accessed October 14, 2014. http://visual.ly/great-divide-workplace-perceptions-Millennials-need-rise-above-get-hired.

Based upon the most recent literature and surveys I've reviewed, a similar survey, if done today, would likely illustrate closer percentages between Millennial and HR responses. Yet many of the 2013 survey respondents are still in the workplace and still hold outdated views on Millennials.

It is important to note that, between 2012 and 2014, web articles on Millennials entering and already in the workplace that covered topics like engagement, productivity, and loyalty (EPL) had titles such as these, "Employers Don't Think Much of Millennials' Work Ethic;" [41] "Millennials at Work: Young and Callow, Like Their Parents;"[42] and

Who Are Millennials? | Welcome to Connected Age

"Millennial Workers: Entitled, Needy, Self-Centered?"[43] Recent articles illustrate that there are still serious issues of misperception, but the titles are much less inflammatory. The reality is, as I've noted from the beginning of this book, nothing is wrong with the Millennials—they are phenomenal vocational talent. The perception issues are due to the collapse of Modern Philosophy and the business model paradigm transformation from Industrial Age to Connected Age workplace environments.

In 2015, a large scale mutigenerational survey by Cangrade, a data science and predictive analytics firm, indicated that Millennials and prior generations shared similar concerns for work-life balance, job security, intellectual stimulation, job preference, and job variation.[44] An article by Michael Marciniak reviewing the Cangrade study identified job variation as a key component of future business adaptations and concludes, "What this means is that we can no longer use one-size fits-all solutions to attract employees, or to keep them happy, satisfied, and productive. Younger generations have diversified as they adapted to modern advances, and businesses will need to do the same to stay competitive."[45]

More and more research was beginning to indicate that there may be greater similarities between the generations than differences. A 5,400-person survey among Baby Boomers, Gen Xers, and Millennials found that they all shared the same five top employer expectations: to be able to work on challenging projects; to have competitive compensation; to have career path opportunities including advancement, learning, and growing in their jobs; to have fair treatment; and to have work-life balance.[46]

A February 2015 public relations article on an IBM study made the observation, "…the hype about Millennial employees simply isn't true. They aren't the 'lazy, entitled, selfish and shallow' workers that many believe them to be."[47] The article went on to say that digital proficiency is the fundamental distinction between Millennials and older generations in the workplace and expectations for things like goals, engagement, leadership preferences, and recognition are equally shared among the generations.[48]

The IBM study was a multigenerational preference and behavioral pattern survey of 1,784 Millennial, Gen-X, and Baby Boomer talent from twelve countries and six industries. Five Millennial patterns typically identified in most articles and included as part of this study include career goals and expectations, attention and reward, digital and professional boundaries, decision-making, and job-hopping. For each of these pattern areas, Millennials were shown to be in balance with other generations in the workforce. Carolyn Heller Baird, the cited author of the IBM study, wrote, "We discovered that Millennials want many of the same things their older colleagues do. While there are some distinctions among the generations, Millennials' attitudes are not poles apart from other employees."[49]

The IBM study did reveal three "uncomfortable truths," as Baird called them:

> Employees are in the dark. Many aren't sure they understand their organization's business strategy—and their leaders are partly to blame... All three generations think the customer experience is poor... Employees of all ages have embraced the technological revolution. The problem? Their enterprises are slow to implement new applications.[50]

These IBM "uncomfortable truths" may reflect the results of a 2014 online survey of 2,100-plus adults over eighteen. Whitney Ricketts wrote that the online survey findings underscore "...a widespread desire of working Americans to leave their current jobs in pursuit of new careers, entrepreneurship, and more creative work. The findings indicate the American workforce is shifting toward work defined by creativity, collaboration, and challenge—away from corporate America."[51]

Joseph Coombs authored a bulletin from the Society of Human Resources summarizing what the workplace faced. He put it this way: "Ultimately, as the makeup of today's workforce changes, HR professionals must adapt accordingly and employ a wide variety of tactics to address the needs of these influential demographic groups."[52] The article focuses on the changing demographic landscape within large corporations that would require a significant human resource transition. Coombs stated the focus as follows, "With repeated waves of Baby Boomers entering retirement, and with members of the larger Millennial generation poised to replace many of those older workers, a cultural shift is at hand that will determine benefits offerings, succession planning, and other aspects of HR's operations."[53]

Once extensive studies concluded the Millennials were not broken, magazine and journal articles by members of the Millennial generation, like Ross Pomeroy and William Handke, responded to the old view of their generation as, "…a classic case of blaming the victim."[54] While the social commentators called the Millennials a lazy cohort of narcissistic brats, these Millennials responded that the economy was the true cause of what was observed of their generation in the past. Pomeroy and Handke wrote, "The Great Recession stymied economic growth, halted job creation, kept older Americans in the workforce longer, and encouraged younger Americans to continue debt-financed schooling."[55]

In another article, B. J. Kito, a Millennial author writes, "Discard the cynical view of Millennials that permeates our culture and behold the truth of the much-maligned generation. It's downright shocking."[56] The articles explained how Millennials support non-profits, a democratic culture, and invest in causes. All of these facts illustrate that Millennials are not "lazy," "stupid," and "the worst."[57]

From 2016 and into 2019, research, articles, and published studies on Millennials at work continued to proliferate with an emphasis on Millennial value in the workplace rather than their liability. Millennials are no longer just the entry-level talent in the workplace with many now having assumed middle management and upper management positions in most organizations and business sectors. As they continue to age and rise in roles and responsibilities, the Industrial Age workplace will soon enter the dustbin of historical ages gone-by, as Connected Age workplaces, reflective of the philosophic, economic, technologic, and pedagogic shifts, arise and occupy the workplace landscape for generations to come.

The Gallup organization published a remarkable and detailed report in 2016, available on-line, entitled, "How Millennials Want to Work and Live."[58] If you want a great picture of where we are and more than I can present in this book, I'd recommend you start there. The Chairman and CEO of Gallup was not exaggerating in his introduction to the report when he writes, " 'Are millennials really that different?' The answer is yes — profoundly so. Millennials will change the world decisively more than any other generation." He summarizes the reasons for his statement and ends with this, "Millennials are changing the very will of the world. So,

Unleash The Millennials and Save the World

we, too, must change. Gallup is recommending that our client partners change their organizational cultures this year from old will to new will. There are six functional changes that we call the 'Big Six.'"[59]

The Gallup "Big Six" is given in a table and expanded upon in their report. The Change in Leadership table is presented below and reflects the soon-to-blossom reality of all workplace environments. What you see in their table is an accurate differentiation between the Industrial Age business model paradigm and Connected Age business model paradigm.

Good news is that many companies have already begun to introduce Connected Age workplace career development and advancement opportunity training into their organizations and are reaping the benefits of Unleashing the Millennials. The use of coaching as the preferred method of Millennial learning and assessment is growing and producing great results. However, there are still many organizations that are still unaware of the situation or are simply refusing to unleash their Millennial talent and transition into the Connected Age paradigm.

Gallup's Six Big Changes Leaders Have To Make	
Past	Future
My Paycheck	My Purpose
My Satisfaction	My Development
My Boss	My Coach
My Annual Review	My Ongoing Conversations
My Weaknesses	My Strengths
My Job	My Life

Clifton, Jim, "How Millennials Want to Work and Live – The Six Big Changes Leaders Have to Make" Gallup.com, last accessed August 19, 2019, https://www.gallup.com/workplace/238073/millennials-work-live.aspx

Who are these Millennials who will rule and why should Boomers help them ascend to their destiny? First, Millennials are the most educated generation in history and trained to work in Connected Age jobs. They not only value but deserve rapid advancement. If you look back over history you will see that the most productive and creative years of talent occurs between ages 19 and 38. This is true for virtually every vocation including literature, science, engineering, art, music, and the list goes on.

Who Are Millennials? | Welcome to Connected Age

While vocational knowledge and wisdom increases beyond these years, the times of greatest creativity and innovation are during these years. Unleash The Millennials in their prime-time and Save the World.

Second, Millennials value and deserve rapid advancement. The Boomers who began entering an Industrial Age workforce back in 1964 have taken us to the end of that Age and cannot complete the transformation into the Connected Age. Boomers still occupying top tier positions must intentionally begin transitioning leadership and responsibilities to Connected Age talent if they want their companies to survive.

Third, Millennials have been trained to communicate, cooperate, collaborate, and co-create (C4) for innovating solutions to Connected Age needs. They desire coaching by older and more experienced vocational experts to help them develop through a transfer of knowledge. There is no longer one source of information or knowledge, rather information and knowledge are an organic collective from many diverse sources. Coaches help Millennial workers accumulate, assimilate, and synthesize disparate information into innovative realities. Boomers holding onto institutional knowledge (IK) as a hedge against displacement will soon discover that the value of IK retained is zero. But the value of IK communicated and innovated by a Millennial is a legacy.

Fourth, Millennials are working Connected Age career paths of work/life balance, regular assessment and feedback. This is not a slacker's road but rather a 24/7 global endeavor with long term sustainability accomplished through informed and methodical steps with many metrics along the way. The key to Millennial success is C4—allowing innovation to flourish. This is not done by work at a desk necessarily but rather is reflective of a lifestyle in which work goals are infused with life goals and supported by flourishing encounters along the way.

Fifth and finally, Millennials are facing what may well be the greatest challenges ever experienced in human history. During the upcoming millennium change, they will need guidance as they enter the gauntlet. The Connected Age has opened Pandora's box on every possible way the demise of humanity could play out. The list of possibilities stretches from genetics to economic currency, the electrical grid or lack thereof, climate change, and even what constitutes life and beyond. Millennials will have to delicately navigate the path forward as artificial intelligence (AI) is

Unleash The Millennials and Save the World

unleashed and the power of knowledge and lack of privacy unhinges any sense of personal safety or global security. Boomers, if you want to ensure your grandchildren have a world to live in, you'd better help Millennials get a grip and allow them to grasp the future with both hands. Unleash The Millennials and Save the World.

By 2025, the previously referenced MCC tsunami will crest and inundate every aspect of private, public, and non-governmental enterprise, bar none. The effect of the crest's tipping point on how enterprises are run, talent managed, and business conducted is already being reported in the literature. The rate of change will be accelerating during this time as more and more Industrial Age Boomers retire from the workforce at all levels and are replaced by some Xers but predominantly Connected Age Millennial talent. As mentioned earlier, there are not enough Xers to fill all the vacancies about to be created and Millennial talent will get the nod whether or not they are prepared for their positions.

Our Postmodern period has reached the end of its cycle and is flailing. The world is waiting for Millennials to rise up and recapture the ideals of transcendent truth and knowability. The world is waiting for Millennials to envision and create a global economy that allows nations to retain their identities while permitting diversity of thought and freedom of trade. The world is waiting for Millennials to rise up and harness technology to protect privacy, secure freedom, and be a tool for human advancement, and protect us from a non-human replacement, cyber tyrant, or terror. The world is waiting for Millennials to rise up and return pedagogy to educating the whole person in what it means to be human and away from indoctrination toward a philosophic ideology. It is time to Unleash The Millennials and let them rise up to accomplish all that they have been raised, educated, and trained to bring to pass, and Save the World. The world is waiting.

So exactly how do we Unleash The Millennials? I'm glad that question finally came up. The next chapter identifies exactly how to do that. In fact, it will explain the most effective method for unleashing all generations for optimal creativity and innovation in the workplace: coaching. Millennials in particular are receptive to and flourish in a coaching relationship as it fits seamlessly within their educational paradigm. Implement coaching today in your workplace to Unleash The Millennials and Save the World.

Chapter 12

Coaching | Most Effective Method to Unleash Millennials

Given all the changes in the workplace as a result of the two "Age" shifts the best method to help Millennials answer "Why and How" questions, take advantage of development opportunities, identify and pursue career path advancement, and achieve work/life balance is through relational internal and/or external coaching. This chapter introduces coaching and its powerful influence on Millennials in the workforce. Coaching is by far the best way to Unleash Millennials to create and innovate a wide open and prosperous future and Save the World.

A 2018 Gallup poll showed that the engagement of U.S. workers was on the rise, and had tied a historic high, set in 2016, of thirty-four percent.[60] The poll also recorded a new low of thirteen percent for actively disengaged workers, down from sixteen and a half percent in 2016. Worker engagement has averaged thirty percent and worker active disengagement has averaged seventeen percent over the past eighteen years, as reported by Gallup. While the Gallup article presented four possible reasons for the engagement numbers, they were confident that seventy percent of the engagement variance was due to managers and team leaders in workplaces recognizing accomplishments as well as the existence of relationships among coworkers and supervisors. "Team leaders influence whether workers are able to use their strengths to do what they do best, give team members recognition for good work, and hold ongoing conversations to coach their employees…The 21st century workforce expects to have a manager who coaches them based on their strengths..."[61]

Coaching is an authentic relationship between coach and client that engages the innermost part of the client and orients their language, empowerment, and alignment of thinking and behavior with their truest motivation driven desires. In a vocational coaching situation where a client is responsible for X, the client will articulate their own intentional actions aligned with their empowerment framework to create their desired results. Alternative actions/results will also be developed for potential challenges that could get in the way. Clients who continue practicing successful actions over time develop sustainable mastery of creating personal and vocational results that actuate desired outcomes throughout their lifetime.

Millennials thrive in a coaching environment as it naturally fits with how they were educated. They have been educated and trained to be curious and play with problems for the enjoyment of learning, master their play with others to produce desired results, and discover outcomes that clearly result from actions taken. These strategies form the epicenter of innovation. It is not necessarily that X was actuated in the example above (and that was the task at hand), but Y and Z also resulted from the actions. And in moments of mindful awareness of leisure as the talent contemplates X, Y, and Z suddenly an "aha" moment of inspiration and revelation occurs, and the talent realizes Z is a total market disrupter. That if Z were pursued it would eliminate the need for X and Y both. Tell me you don't want that kind of thinking going on in your organization and I'll tell you your organization won't be in business after the next market disruption hits.

As I've previously emphasized, the culture of the traditional Industrial Age workplace is not prepared to effectively use the unique skill sets of Millennial talent. These unique skills are associated with the Connected Age pedagogy with which Millennials were raised and educated. Coaching provides the perfect tools and methods to bridge generational and cultural gaps among Millennials and older generations in the workplace.

Millennials were educated for positions and jobs not yet invented at the time secondary teachers were preparing them. They were taught to ask "Why and How" things are done. They were taught to recognize and know the What; it is obvious and intuitive. The "Why" refers to the

Coaching | Most Effective Method to Unleash Millennials

motivation behind something being done not just because someone said so. And the How refers to the method of achieving the What. Coaching is a relationship that helps talent discover on their own the "Why's" and How's of everything they encounter.

Coaching as a profession was introduced in the early 1980s and by the early 2000s had been proven as a "best method" learning tool for personal and leadership development in the executive C-Suites of the world's largest companies. Coaching has slowly been working its way down the hierarchy in corporations and finally began hitting Millennials around 2016. As a professional practice, it is considered the second fastest growing service industry in the world with over 53,000 certified coaches worldwide and nearly $3 billion in global revenue. This number does not include a much higher number of non-certified coaches who are working internally within corporations.

Coaching, as you will see, is a Connected Age learning process which seamlessly matches up with Millennial learning preferences. The literature is full of positive stories of enhanced engagement, productivity, and loyalty of Millennials who are actively involved in vocational-based coaching relationships. Plus, many large companies with much talent in singular locations have started to introduce entirely new sections in their HR learning departments dedicated specifically to coaching.

Included in this chapter will be an overview of coaching in general, support for coaching from the literature, and reasons why you should start coaching today. There have been innumerable books published that describe the coaching "process", so I have limited my process comments to just a few. While the process is simple generically, it takes a bit more than what I've presented herein to fully comprehend and implement. For quickest results, simply hire a business experienced professional certified coach (PCC) and get started. The rest comes pretty naturally.

The Center for Creative Leadership is one of the top ranked providers of executive education in the world. In their book, The CCL Handbook of Coaching, they define the general field of coaching as follows: "Coaching is first and foremost a way to facilitate learning. For leaders and managers at all levels and in all kinds of organizations, the most powerful lessons arise from experience.... Coaching is an effective tool that can be used to help people learn from their experience."[62]

Unleash The Millennials and Save the World

A rich and informative academic research paper described the effectiveness of coaching as follows: "The results show that coaching has significant positive effects on performance and skills, well-being, coping, work attitudes, and goal-directed self-regulation. In general, our meta-analytic findings indicate that coaching is an effective tool for improving the functioning of individuals in organizations."[63]

The appearance of an entirely new industry (i.e. coaching) that is also the second fastest growing service industry in the world is a simultaneous effect of the philosophic collapse and business model paradigm transformation that resulted in the formation of the Millennial generation. A 2012 article on coaching noted five contributing factors of coaching growth: 1. changing values of people; 2. the demise of the world of traditional work; 3. career choices now both "inner" and "outer" games; 4. traditional education not preparing people for jobs today; and 5. coaching now considered education.[64] The first four factors above align respectively with the shifts in philosophy, economics, technology, and pedagogy. The fifth factor aligns with the change from the Industrial Age to the Connected Age. Coaching is not here by accident as it is the best practice learning tool for generations to come in the Connected Age.

Coaching is currently an unregulated profession with no federal or state standards. This is bad and good. Bad because without regulatory oversight of some form there are no guidelines for what constitutes the minimum standard for coaching. Anyone can call themselves a coach without any experience or training. This is common, so beware. But what is bad is also good, in that you can develop coaches to your own standard within your organization that do not require outside certification.

As business demand for external coaches increased and people started spending time and resources to become coaches, it became evident for both businesses and coaches that a reputable certifying body for coaching was needed. At least three coaching associations jumped in early and are continuing to work toward developing credible, reliable, and valid models for best practices accreditation.[65] They include the International Coach Federation (ICF), the Worldwide Association of Business Coaches (WABC), and the International Association of Coaching (IAC). Each of these membership-based organizations uses similar approaches for providing their own specific content-based criteria and standards for curriculum to be used in coaching schools applying for their accreditation.

Approved and accredited coaching schools train the students who apply to the appropriate associations for certification.[66]

Real challenges exist for these three associations, as well as the myriad of other less organized associations that also proclaim accreditation authority. These challenges include who accredits the accreditors; assessments for accreditation are not disclosed; self-accreditation can be a conflict of interest; and how well accreditation actually contributes to the quality of the coaching being offered.[67]

While there are myriad coaching "programs" that cover the gamut of applications, there are only a few research-based and accredited coaching "models" for how to conduct coaching (i.e. the process). Let me introduce two such models.

The Center for Creative Leadership (CCL) provides the most widely recognized model. The coaching framework for CCL is explained in their Leadership Coaching Services brochure as follows: "CCL's coaching model, called RACSR™, is a comprehensive, researched-based, dynamic framework. The five key components of this model, when used in proper proportion, guide the coaching engagement, and produce optimal personal and professional results."[68] The CCL coaching components expressed in their acronym RACSR starts with a firmly grounded relationship (R). Within this relationship context are their three core elements for coaching: assessment (A), challenge (C), and support (S). As the core elements are worked through over time during a coaching relationship, both direct and indirect outcomes that are in line with the goals of the coaching are achieved by results (R).

Coachville, one of the world's largest coach training providers and where I received my ICF-approved training, uses the acrostic RACE to identify the framework of their model for the coaching relationship. In this model, also encompassed in a safe and engaged coach/client relationship, they create results (R) through specific actions (A) in an environment of challenges (C) that are regularly assessed by evaluation (E).[69] Through this process, skills are developed, mastery is attained, and the individual can become a new person from the inside out.

So, what exactly is coaching? I use two definitions when introducing people unfamiliar with coaching to the process and intent. The first is generic and the second particular to coaching in the workplace environment. While the process is the same across the full spectrum of coaching, specific applications, such as the workplace, have their nuances.

Coaching defined: The field of coaching is a Socratic type inquiry-based relationship between a coach and client who together through authentic, clear, and judgment-free, present-moment awareness and communication discover client motivations for the things they want to accomplish or overcome. Client motivations are articulated in direct response to masterfully interwoven, appropriate, inquisitive, and provocative questions that elicit answers found hidden in the recesses of the client's mind and heart. Once articulated, these same motivations endow clients with an inspired ability to assimilate, align, and synthesize intentional actions for creating desired results toward conceiving their life purpose, actuating their vision, and giving rise to their legacy/destiny.

Vocational coaching defined: Vocational coaching is a Socratic type inquiry-based relationship between a coach and an employee who, through authentic, clear, and judgment-free present-moment awareness and communication discover together the motivations for work and the tools they use. A worker's motivations are articulated in direct response to masterfully interwoven, appropriate, inquisitive, and provocative questions regarding language, empowerment, and alignment (LEA) in the workplace that elicit answers found in the worker's mind and heart. Once a person's individual vocational LEA is recognized, he or she can align, assimilate, and synthesize actions for discovering life meaning, individual purpose, and vocational calling by optimizing their engagement, productivity, and loyalty in the workplace. Over time, mastery in sustainable vocational/professional development occurs, followed by increased opportunities for advancement.

I am convinced that Socrates was right on the mark when he said the unexamined life is not worth living. We often go through life unsatisfied and half-hearted, even while accomplishing Herculean feats, because our external efforts are done to impress or satisfy others, thus creating internal angst. Opening the gateway to sustainable satisfaction and joy in conceiving life purpose and achieving one's vision is through authenticity and vulnerability. Coaching is a relationship where the client is provided a safe, judgment-free environment with a trusted coach. Coaching clients, in that safe setting, can articulate what is on their minds and in their hearts.

Coaching | Most Effective Method to Unleash Millennials

Isn't it interesting that Millennials raised in a culture engaged in a raucous verbal war over transcendent truth and knowability would have as their hearts' desire to discover their own life meaning and individual purpose so as to pursue their vocational calling? And at the same time, as they entered an Industrial Age workplace, they demonstrated a character seemingly void of engagement, productivity, and loyalty? Do you now begin to see the two are intimately tied together? They were educated to play, master, and discover and entered an Industrial Age workplace that was task-based, outcome oriented, and goal focused with no play, no mastery, no discovery, just work, work, work. As this concept begins to take root in your mind it will begin to grow and reveal to you the extent of the productivity-through-coaching that can be demonstrated in a right-fitted workplace environment. We have produced a generation whose passion is pursuing beautiful, optimal, creative, and innovative productivity that benefits not just themselves but all who inhabit this beautiful planet we call Earth. Unleash The Millennials and Save the World.

In a vocational setting, there are three major areas where Millennials are empowered: technical – specific daily work (i.e. the doers); business of the business – enterprise operations (i.e. group leaders); and management – relationships & soft skills (i.e. leadership & HR). Vocational coaching takes into account both the talent's motivations and the motivations behind why the employer has empowered the client in these areas. The coach's role is to help talent envision what motivates and empowers them and align their actions accordingly. When done properly, intentional action in sync with empowerment boosts engagement and productivity.

Coaching is based on an authentic relationship between coaches and clients that engages them and orients their essential language, empowerment, and alignment of thinking and behavior with their truest motivation-driven desires. In a vocational coaching situation where talent is responsible for X, he or she will articulate the intentional actions aligned with personal empowerment to create desired results. Alternative actions/results will also be developed for potential challenges that could get in the way. Coached talent who continue practicing successful actions over time develop sustainable mastery, achieve personal and vocational results that bring about desired outcomes throughout their lifetime. Coaching flat-out works!

Unleash The Millennials and Save the World

The observations of Millennial talent are that work within the Industrial Age environment is not fun, does not answer their question of purpose, and does not make sufficient allowance for personal time to create work/life balance. Coaching of all generations in the workplace provides the human touch that allows outdated perceptions of Millennials to be dispelled. Through open dialogue, free expression, and the resolution of differences of opinion, people in the workplace understand one another much better. Coaching is designed to identify milestones and establish the means of measurement that would indicate progress for the individual being coached. While not perfect, coaching can allow individuals to experience sustainable achievement and empowerment in all areas if they choose to continue in the process.

There has been a lot of literature written about coaching Millennials so let me share a few examples of what others are saying about this practice. Several of these examples also mention mentoring, which still has its place. Consider the following cited quotations.

> Unlike generations prior, Millennials want to see their managers as coaches and mentors and admire experience and knowledge over position and power.[70]

> ...[O]nce they're hired [Millennials], expect to work for a supervisor who will coach and guide them along a career path.... [D]on't assume they want this kind of coaching over email. Our research indicates they're looking for face-to-face consultation where they can get sound advice and answers to their specific questions.[71]

> Enhance performance management systems with new tools to help employees navigate their careers... to identify a wider range of job opportunities throughout the company, and to offer more 'just-in-time' feedback and coaching.[72]

> Offer coaching and mentoring programs to encourage cross-generational communication and enhance career satisfaction.[73]

Coaching | Most Effective Method to Unleash Millennials

> One survey found that 80 percent of Millennials said they wanted regular feedback from their managers, and 75 percent longed for mentors.[74]
>
> Millennials rely more on formal training and mentoring to develop their skills... Millennials want informal feedback from their managers 50% more often than older peers.[75]
>
> Improving your company's ability to give employees honest, timely, and useful coaching won't benefit just your 20-something workers."[76]

Perhaps most shocking in light of all the above quotations is that giving feedback was ranked "dead last" in eight manager competence skills (i.e. 8th of 8 competencies) in a ranking by HR professionals of their managers' confidence.[77] In other words managers today are not seen by HR professionals to be trained, equipped, or required to give the regular feedback Millennial talent wants and needs. I hope this section has demonstrated that coaching does fill this feedback void, and, in the next chapter, I'll show you how to get started.

Deloitte Touche Tohmatsu Limited (Deloitte) of the UK published the results of a survey they conducted with 7,800 Millennial respondents from twenty-six countries in North American and Latin America, Western Europe and Asia-Pacific. The Executive Summary report for the survey notes, "Millennials, who are already emerging as leaders in technology and other industries and will comprise 75 percent of the global workforce by 2025, want to work for organizations that foster innovative thinking, develop their skills, and make a positive contribution to society."[78] This study also reveals that Millennials do not believe businesses are currently doing as much as they can to develop their leadership skills. The report states, "Almost one in four Millennials are 'asking for a chance' to show their leadership skills. Additionally, 75 percent believe their organizations could do more to develop future leaders."[79] And as shown in the string of quotes previously, coaching is a key element of what future leaders want in terms of development.

Unleash The Millennials and Save the World

For coaching Millennials, I have found Coachville's RACE model extremely effective in that it is centered around play to develop mastery. The initial step is for talent to name a game for something they would like to accomplish that has a specific purpose. The process of naming the game is done with "purpose" in mind so as the name and purpose coincide. This is a critical and also fun beginning as it gives the talent a touchstone of why they are doing what they are doing. Next the talent identifies the objectives of the game in terms of tangible achievements, skills to improve, and character traits to build. Playing involves doing something so the talent identifies the recurring activities and frequencies of activities they envision and the challenges they may face while playing. And of course, successful actions create results, so the talent identifies those results that indicate winning of the game is occurring. To WIN the game is to actuate outcomes from results that fulfill the purpose for why the game was played.

As the talent drills down on their recurring activities, they identify the strengths and talents needed for success and develop a strategy for gaining and/or improving these strengths and talents and prepare a game plan to do so. The strategy would include the practice of specific skills that help them develop mastery.

In regard to challenges often it is the talents internal resistance to engage the challenge that is the bigger hurdle than the challenge itself. Thru vulnerability exercises talent realigns their healthy emotional integration and successfully resolve challenges to creating results. And finally, the talent identifies those personal environmental assets and obstacles such as ideas, people, places, and things. Moving forward they use the assets they have while eliminating the obstacles and filling in the gaps.

As mentioned earlier, companies have been successfully bringing in external coaches and hiring internal coaches to work with their talent. Coaching is no longer considered a luxury by many but a necessary and functional part of the fabric of their cultural and talent. If you are exploring how to bring coaching into your organization keep two things in mind. First, identify your labor percentage versus the total revenue produced by that labor. And second, identify who will be involved with overseeing coaching provided within the organization. In regard to the first point, there are two main reasons we do not professionally develop

Coaching | Most Effective Method to Unleash Millennials

our vocational workforce talent: 1) Our talent is too busy making money for the company to be trained; and 2) Our talent is not busy and is costing the company money. In either case, financial and support resources for training are rarely allocated.

The top driver for Millennial engagement, productivity, and loyalty is career development and opportunities for advancement. Rather than thinking there is no good time to train your Millennial talent, think in terms of training is not optional; and training during peak business periods is optimal. Productivity is the key metric for optimizing output with revenue to right size your labor burden. And coaching is a productivity superpower that only costs a fraction of the return you'll get when Millennial engagement, productivity, and loyalty (EPL) are optimized.

During peak business periods profit margins are higher than normally experienced as revenue extends operating income well beyond your normal break-even costs. To the casual observer these excess profits seem offensive/obscene; to the owners they are windfalls; to the operational personnel an opportunity for profit sharing; to the IT executive they are an opportunity to upgrade technology; to the CEO/President they are an opportunity to invest in developing their people for innovation and taking the company to the next level. As the discussions on what to do with excess profits during peak periods occur at the C-suite level or in your small business remember one simple thing—Millennials are your future and providing them vocational development learning tools such as coaching is a no brainer if you want them to create and innovate for continued peak business metrics with sustainable growth.

With the business matters out of the way, and they always get in the way when talking about talent development, we'll look at the second point of who should oversee the coaching program and who the coaches would be. I highly recommend your Coaching Director be a senior executive leader in the organization or an experienced outside Professional Certified Coach (PCC). Coaching will directly impact operational elements of the business given it enables talent to fully grasp what they are doing and engage fully in optimizing their actions and results. If something structurally or in the fabric of the organization is not working or out of balance talent being coached will identify it and begin processes to work around or touch the workplace framework to resolve impediments to achieving results. It is imperative that a senior executive with empowerment over the framework has direct oversight and is supportive of the coaching being conducted for it to be successful.

Your coaches will be training up Connected Age Millennial talent who have the potential of absolutely disrupting the status quo of the older workforce. This disruption will result from their unequaled engagement, optimal productivity, and undivided loyalty as they strive to transparently communicate, cooperate, collaborate, and co-create innovative growth in the organization by just "doing their jobs." The role of the senior executive is to make sure the older and more experienced workforce talent do not feel threatened but rather joins in the process of communicating, cooperating, collaborating, and cocreating (C4) with the Millennial coached talent. And together to take the company above and beyond everyone's wildest imaginations of enterprise success.

This Coaching Director's role cannot effectively be filled by an in-house trainer or other HR talet, but it could be your senior HR executive. The inhouse trainer and HR talent are not as empowered as the senior executive who speaks, and people listen and are calmed and willingly participate. Your in-house trainer and/or HR talent can and should act as coaches and administrators of the coaching program and do many of the day to day duties under the Director's authorization and supervision.

An outside PCC reporting directly to a senior executive can also fill this Coaching Director's role and be supported by internal training and HR talent. In this scenario the outside PCC would be empowered by a senior executive to act in their capacity. The outside PCC provides a sense of independence to all talent in the workforce and the understanding that he or she is answerable to a senior executive who is really running the show.

Many companies are currently using both internal and external coaches in their organizations. For internal coaches, it is best if the coaches are older, experienced workforce talent who have the personality, temperament, and desire to coach co-workers. Workforce coaches need to be trained in the coaching process and be coached themselves during their initial year to get them intimately familiar not just with the process but the results of coaching.

If you use an outside coach, like me (full transparency), it is best to hire an experienced PCC coach who is certified by industry-recognized associations and who can commit to their own engagement in the

Coaching | Most Effective Method to Unleash Millennials

coaching program. The coaching relationship is "everything," so you don't want to have multiple coaches for the same person. As mentioned earlier, there is no regulatory standard for coaching, and anyone can say, "I'm a coach." In order to get industry recognized Professional Certified Coach designation by an industry-recognized association (e.g. ICF), there are significant, objectively measured training courses, coaching practicums, and standardized testing that need to be completed. In addition, certified coaches are to uphold formal codes of conduct and ethical standards and earn continuing education credits to maintain certification. This does not mean a non-certified coach cannot be as masterful as a PCC in practice, but you just need to be sure you really know and trust them. Coaches are closely engaged with your talent, who are the core of your business. I encourage you not to hand your talent over to someone who does not know how to coach.

Outside coaches should consult with appropriate operational personnel after each coaching session and ensure what talent have proposed falls within the workplace framework of expectations. In these consultations, coaching confidences between talent and coach must be maintained. Coaching is a relationship of keeping confidences within the relationship, therefore, during these coaching debriefs with operational personnel the confidences disclosed within the session will not be disclosed. Rather, the coach will present their need for clarification in such a way as to obtain the information they need to be confident talent can proceed with a planned course of actions. If the coach deems it warranted, they will suggest to talent that they should seek internal counsel before proceeding.

You've heard me mention engagement, productivity, and loyalty (EPL) repeatedly in this book. I will spend the next three chapters defining and addressing EPL. I'll also discuss "enhancement drivers" which provide maximum effect in the workplace. EPL is what keeps you in business, so enhancing it goes right to the bottom line.

The top workplace drivers for EPL the past ten years are vocational development, career path advancement opportunities, and work/life balance. And key to a Millennials desire for development, advancement, and work/life balance is the discovery of life meaning, purpose, and calling. More incredibly, all these terms/factors are intimately related. Simply put, there are three tiered trifectas of intimate connection.

Unleash The Millennials and Save the World

Engagement leads to development which gives life meaning. Productivity leads to advancement which reveals life purpose. Loyalty leads to work/life balance which affirm vocational calling. See table below.

	Three Tiered Trifecta of Life, Meaning, and Purpose		
	Trifecta 1	**Trifecta 2**	**Trifecta 3**
Tier 1	Engagement	Productivity	Loyalty
Tier 2	Development	Advancement	Work/Life Balance
Tier 3	Life Meaning	Life Purpose	Life Calling

It is through EPL that Millennials will develop, advance, and achieve work/life balance as they transition their work environments to Connected Age workspaces in preparation for the millennium change cycle (MCC) tsunami surge and aftermath. And throughout this sustainable process of development, advancement, and balance, Millennials will illuminate knowing their lives have meaning and purpose, and their vocational pursuit is not just a job by a calling.

Let's remind ourselves what the 2016 Gallup survey report indicated were the six most important cultural drivers in the Connected Age workplace: My Purpose; My Development; My Coach; My Ongoing Conversations; My Strengths; and My Life. These are the issues being discussed at workplace transformation conferences. They need to be addressed in Industrial Age workplaces. Let's look more closely at what EPL is and why a company can demonstrate transformation in engagement, productivity, and loyalty as talent discovers life meaning, purpose, and calling in their workplace. We'll then look at what drives EPL for Millennials in the workplace today.

The importance of these next three chapter is not necessarily the definitions and explanations. The focus is on the reality all facets of EPL work together organically in and around a person making each Millennial talent unique and an important asset individually and in team environments. Unleash The Millennials and Save the World.

Chapter 13

Engagement | Life Meaning and Drivers for Development

My definition for engagement is, "A sustainable level of high performance beneficial to both employer and employee." Being engaged is step one of a fulfilling work experience that also produces best results. The emotional commitment of a worker and their empowerment to perform are intimately associated with engagement. Engagement occurs most naturally within a supportive workplace where there is open and transparent communication, cooperation, collaboration, and co-creation (C4) and in which outcomes are clearly articulated, regularly measured and evaluated, and feedback is provided.

Engaged talent are recognized by their high involvement level and enthusiasm about what they do and where they work. They "own" their work and are the ones who push the organizational momentum forward in performance and innovation. Organizations that are best at getting talent engaged achieve four times the earnings growth than their competitors.[80] And engagement all starts with alignment.

Alignment individually addresses people, positions, and career path opportunities. Consistent alignment is the practice of intentionally getting various shaped pegs into and through holes that best match them. Perfect alignment is an aspiration; extremely rare if not impossible. Alignment is achieved by using appropriate standardized and research-based assessments that identify personality profile and temperament (Myers Briggs, DISC, Strength-Finder, Hogan, Enneagram, etc.) and by evaluating their findings. The results of the assessments should be used

Unleash The Millennials and Save the World

to ensure a match between talent and their duties/job descriptions. If there is not a match engagement will suffer. Consistently reassess job alignment, because as people evolve their job alignment may decrease, and duties need to change. Finally, identify career path opportunities for advancement as a result of successful engagement in the position by the person.

For the Industrial Age workplace engagement has historically been thought of as merely doing your job. But for the Millennial they are not just doing a job but living an emotionally integrated and emboldened Connected Age life of which work is merely a part. When any person experiences satisfaction, appreciation, and recognition that they are making a positive difference by engaging in what they do at work life meaning in the workplace becomes pretty self-evident. And beyond the workplace life meaning continues as they similarly engage their own life.

When work or life conditions make emotional commitment to engage difficult and/or when empowerment in a high stress position is vague, talent will either leave to pursue other options or slog it out because they need the money now. Eventually those Millennials that stick around will become resentful of the waste of their precious time that cannot be recovered engaging in work in where they find little or no meaning.

Empowerment is the process of becoming stronger and more confident, especially in guiding one's own life. In the workplace, being empowered includes having responsibility and authority. At lower levels, defining responsibility and authority can be fairly simple. As workers move up the ladder, workplace friction is common when areas of empowerment begin to overlap among people in the same workplace. Empower all personnel to utilize communication, cooperation, collaboration, and co-creation in order to help them recognize areas of overlap and, when conflict arises, seek resolution.

This is not just for Millennials but for all generations as we all spend most of our adult lives until retirement working in some capacity. Just look at the number of articles being written today trying to help the retired Boomers find meaning in retirement. The number of articles reflects the reality that Boomers like all past generations that worked hard until retirement, are finding it difficult to find life meaning after satisfactory engagement at work stopped. And a frequent suggestion for Boomers is to serve others where satisfaction and meaning are experienced by most.

Engagement | Life Meaning and Drivers for Development

Talent engagement is commonly broken up into three buckets, engaged, not-engaged, and actively disengaged. The bucket containing those identified as not-engaged typically has the majority percentage of workplace talent. The other two buckets, engaged and actively disengaged, have historically contained nearly equal percentages of the remaining talent. Gallup noted a positive percentage shift in the two smaller buckets in a 2018 engagement poll that noted thirty-four percent were of U.S. workers were engaged, fifty-three percent were not engaged, and thirteen percent were actively disengaged.[81]

Talent that is not engaged are recognized by a lack of enthusiasm about what they do and where they work. They may be on time, glad to have the position, do their job well, and produce their daily quota but all with low energy and lack of passion. And once the work-day is finished what they're working on doesn't come to mind until they return the next day. Some people call the not engaged talent "worker bees" and suggest every organization needs them. I think many are just misaligned with who they are and what they are doing at work. Alignment opportunities may not be possible, but they need the money, so they keep working in a less than meaningful position.

There may be some who are not engaged because they sense a lack of engagement opportunity in their current position or company. Getting the not engaged who desire engagement to become engaged benefits an organization at every level of measurement including: improved customer interactions, productivity gains, less turnover, reduced on the job accidents, improved talent health, and profit increases over twenty-one percent.[82] These not engaged may have an idea where their best fit for alignment would be but openings or opportunities are not available. How many great chefs have gone undiscovered because they were hired as an assistant cook but discovered upon arrival that their waiting tables was a higher priority for the manager. Get your not engaged aligned properly and see how high they can fly.

While you work to improve engagement and inclusion of the not engaged through alignment you also need to seriously assess and address your talent that is actively disengaged. Actively disengaged talent are not merely unhappy they're miserable and resentful about work and proactively use actions and influence to destroy their engaged coworkers efforts. These individuals find no satisfaction in their work and life meaning at work is unbearable. It is estimated the actively disengaged cost U.S. business between $480 to $600 billion each year in lost productivity.[83] The generation noted in a 2016 Gallup study on Millennials to have the highest active disengagement are not Millennials but Boomers at nineteen percent.[84]

That means statistically one out of five Boomers are actively disengaged at work. I'm sure you could name exactly who they are in your office as you read this. And here's the sad thing. They know it, don't care if you know it, and are just waiting for someone to say something so they can go off on them about how totally miserable they really are. I encourage empathy in many of their cases as the older you get the more life issues arise (i.e. deaths, divorce, financial mistakes, isolation, etc.) that can literally sap away over time all sense of joy and hope about work and life. While empathetic, you cannot allow them to continue their active disengagement in the workplace. If they have value and are willing, realign them in their current position or in a new position. A reengaged Boomer that was once actively disengaged teamed up with a sharp Millennial can become one of your strongest assets as the Boomer knows where all your weak spots are and what not to do; they've been plowing that field for quite a while. Teams of reengaged Boomers with institutional wisdom and Connected Age mindset Millennials are an unstoppable combination.

Over the last 15 years there have been mountains of studies and articles written which initially focused on getting Millennials to engage work in general and most recently they have been focused on specific drivers that enhance their engagement in the workplace. The primary area of focus in the literature for initial Millennial engagement was emotional commitment. In 2019, the top engagement drivers for engagement, productivity, and loyalty (EPL) were vocational development, career path advancement opportunities, and work/life balance. In the intervening time between the earliest and lasted literature reviewed significant transformation in the workplace has occurred as Industrial Age business model companies have given way to Connected Age business model companies.

Here are just a few examples of the types of emotional engagement quotes that were appearing in print. "This emotional commitment means engaged employees actually care about their work and their company. They don't work just for a paycheck, or just for the next promotion, but

Engagement | Life Meaning and Drivers for Development

work on behalf of the organization's goals."[85] "Employee engagement is a workplace approach designed to ensure that employees are committed to their organization's goals and values, motivated to contribute to organizational success, and are able at the same time to enhance their own sense of well-being."[86] "Engaged organizations have strong and authentic values, with clear evidence of trust and fairness based on mutual respect, where two way promises and commitments—between employers and staff—are understood, and are fulfilled."[87]

Emotional commitment is a very fluid thing that can range from healthy to dysfunctional. When people are in close proximity personal relationships of dysfunction that directly impact every aspect of the involved individuals' lives forms an extremely strong enmeshment bond of survival loyalty. This type of enmeshment loyalty bond is irrespective of person, gender, social class, family of origin, organization affiliation, or nature of dysfunction. Dysfunction is not the type of emotional commitment you want to have in your organization, but these types of commitments do exist and are important to mention.

A 2018 article in the International Journal of Business Administration published a paper on the results of a qualitative researched based study conducted within a single large and significant organization. The paper is entitled "Dysfunctional Behavior at the Workplace and Its Impact on Employees."[88] The paper focused on three main areas: concepts and types of dysfunctional behavior, individual and organizational consequences, and job performance. In addition to causing the types of consequences you'd expect from dysfunctional behavior including low job performance and reduced productivity, the number one consequence was lack of company loyalty and high turnover. The top dysfunctional behaviors identified included: attitude problems, organizational problems, insecurities, poor performance, and communication problems.[89]

What interested me about the study and reason for mentioning it is the culture of the organization in the study was intentionally focused on their core guiding principles of Sustainable Development and Human Consciousness. As a result of the study findings the recommendations stated, "It is recommended that ___ [Note: I purposely left out company name] begin to take new approaches to seriously tackle managerial issues with the same focus as it does cultural issues."[90] The conclusions stated, "It is important to note that despite all of the social innovations established by ___, and despite placing the human at the center of the organization, common issues of organizational dysfunction still managed to crop upon in and around the organization."[91] The company had a very employee centered and proactive cultural focus yet the management within the company was not implementing that culture at the individual level. The employees were stoked about the company culture but were being burned by their supervisors and unchecked peers. Make sure your desired company culture matches your supervisors' actions to infuse that culture at the individual employee level and to immediately identify and address instances of dysfunction.

A healthy emotional commitment is one where the talent experiences a common affirmation of importance in position from the company, their supervisor, and their peers of their own individual engagement contributions to their team, the teams' group, and the company. This affirmation comes both directly and indirectly as a result of proper alignment for their position (skills, personality, temperament, duties, and desire) which enhances engagement and actions taken in their position to actuate desired results and outcomes which enhances productivity.

Millennials are not looking for easy but rather vocational pursuits that would allow them to play and develop mastery and the opportunity to produce results and outcomes that would help open career path opportunities. They recognize more than any previous generation in the workforce today that vocational work is a major part of their life but not their whole life. A healthy emotional commitment is one where Millennials recognize a desirable part of their life is being engaged and productive in meaningful work at your company as affirmed by the company, their supervisor, and peers.

They have been encouraged to be emotionally and meaningfully connected with their parents, teachers, peers, administrators, and coaches, all of whom work together to prepare them for future success in the college and career of their choosing. This same encouragement continued on college campuses where students, peers, faculty, and administrators work together for the individualized success of each student in a Connected Age endeavor.

When Millennials first began entering the workplace, these same emotionally integrated students accepted positions in Industrial Age companies and were supervised by emotionally disengaged Boomers who

Engagement | Life Meaning and Drivers for Development

just wanted someone to do the job. It was not a pretty scene between 2008 and 2014. However, beginning in 2015 enough Millennials were in the workforce that emotional engagement as a factor in engagement and job satisfaction began to be widely recognized. Connected Age businesses actively began introducing coaching as a foundational emotional engagement bridge to span the gap between Millennials and their Boomer supervisors. And then Millennials began to engage and make huge strides in advancing the businesses they were part of by changing the culture to be more open to communication, cooperation, collaboration, and co-creation (C4).

Business is not mechanical but personal. Boomers in a sense were mechanical in their emotions thus there was some confusion when real emotionally integrated Millennial talent began to enter. When a relational workplace where emotionally integrated talent is properly nurtured and maintained business growth can become exponential. And when the emotionally integrated talent is not properly nurtured and maintained the business can develop dysfunctional symptoms and experience loss of engagement and decay.

This idea of a relational workplace environment driving engagement is not something new. In 2008, the United Kingdom (UK) funded a massive study entitled, "Engaging for Success: Enhancing Performance through Employee Engagement." The four key engagement drivers based on their research were leadership, management, employees, and belief.[92] Leadership of an entity is to ensure absolute transparency of the explicit organizational culture that allows talent to see clearly the relationship between their job and the ultimate vision and goals of the organization. Management is to be engaging and openly providing clarity, talent validation and recognition for their contribution and effort, treatment of people as individuals, appropriate steps to have all work organized such that employees feel valued, and adequate equipping and support for each individual so that they can do their job.[93]

The UK study also noted employees must be stakeholders in their jobs and as such be able to openly voice their ideas and be heard in regard to individual responsibilities as well as the decisions made on behalf of their department. In addition, the organization should help create an atmosphere of cooperation to resolve problems, challenges, and commitments at hand. The employee's trust and sense of security is tied directly to their belief that the organization is true to its values and that what it presents as behavioral norms are actually followed.[94]

The plethora of literature between 2012 to 2015 from other global and smaller studies validated the UK study just cited and present engagement emotional commitment driver suggestions such as: work culture, flexibility, full transparency, community, global mobility, contingent workforce strategy, connection with people, and generational specific strategies.[95] Focusing on engagement levels, selection of right managers, coaching managers and holding them accountable for engagement, defining realistic engagement goals, finding ways to connect with each employee, and developing employee strengths.[96] Inspiration, transparency, and peer-to-peer engagement.[97]

SAS for several years occupied one of the top spots in the Fortune list of Top 100 Best Companies to Work For in the U.S. Writing of the benefits of emotional ties of employees to SAS, Mark Crowley writes, "They've [SAS] discovered that feelings and emotions are the true drivers of employee loyalty, innovation, and productivity, and purposely have made workforce happiness one of their primary missions."[98] SAS has discovered that being a benevolent and respectful organization that demonstrates routinely that their employees matter and are individually valued consistently produces optimal workplace performance. Crowley notes, "This understanding alone could provide the antidote to the country's long-enduring engagement ailment."[99]

The four leadership values that set SAS apart in being a great and productive place to work included: valuing people above all else, giving to employees which results in their giving back, maintaining a culture of trust, and ensuring employees understand their work is significant.[100] Crowley noted, "SAS workers are surveyed on the characteristics of trust proven to be most influential on engagement: open communication, respect from fellow employees, transparency into career-paths, and being treated as a human being."[101]

The emotional component of engagement is applicable for all generations in the workplace. Giving talent opportunities to do what they do best in harmony with the company mission and purpose, opportunities to learn and grow, and knowing supervisors care are all important strategies to engaging and retaining the company's best employees.[102]

Engagement | Life Meaning and Drivers for Development

Two of the key drivers since 2015 have been the reputation and culture of an organization. If you're cool with a poor reputation and for being a sweat shop that doesn't care for their talent, don't expect to hire the best and brightest, or be surprised with high turnover. If you're after the best and brightest Millennials you must have a genuine passion about what you do and how you care for your people. While your "perks" may be nice (who doesn't like perks), the Millennials think beyond the perks and the reality of having to work for you and your organization.

A 2016 Gallup survey noted in their executive summary, "Millennials are less engaged in the workplace than are their older counterparts, and they are more likely to be categorized as 'not engaged.' Millennials' lack of engagement costs the U.S. economy hundreds of billions of dollars annually in lost productivity."[103] Based upon more recent articles and survey results I postulate this comment is still a remnant of the Industrial Age demise while the Connected Age workplaces rise. The more recent survey results and articles appearing since 2017 indicate a pretty dramatic positive shift in the perception and reality of both Millennial engagement and productivity in the workplace.

As mentioned earlier, a 2018 Gallup report presented four possible contributing factors for the engagement numbers measured, they were confident that seventy percent of the positive engagement variance was due to manager and team leader quality in workplace environments that recognized accomplishments and where relationships with coworkers and supervisors exist. "Team leaders influence whether workers are able to use their strengths to do what they do best, give team members recognition for good work, and hold ongoing conversations to coach their employees…The 21st century workforce expects to have a manager who coaches them based on their strengths…"[104]

The most recent 2018 and early 2019 Millennial surveys and articles indicate the top engagement drivers for Millennials are vocational development, career path advancement opportunities, and work/life balance. Companies that have discovered this are using coaching as the best practice method for both helping Millennial talent discover professional development options within an organization and discern those that best fit and are aligned with their skill set and envisioned career path advancement.

Unleash The Millennials and Save the World

This aforementioned 2018 Gallup survey is significant in that it validates statistically what has been recognized in the research for years; interpersonal relationships in the workplace are what drive engagement. The cultural shifts and generational differences in the workplace which have been hindering relationships between generations in the workplace as previously noted are being overcome through coaching which establishes clear communicative, cooperative, collaborative and cocreative (C4) environments.

If executive and managerial leaders do not immediately step up and provide the financial and resource backing to foster emotional engagement of their Millennial staff their business will likely not be in business in five years. The Chairman and CEO of Gallup put it this way, "As this report shows, millennials will continue to disrupt how the world communicates — how we read and write and relate. Millennials are disrupting retail, hospitality, real estate and housing, transportation, entertainment and travel, and they will soon radically change higher education."[105] Get ready, the future is here today! Unleash The Millennials and Save the World.

Chapter 14

Productivity | Life Purpose and Drivers for Advancement

Employee productivity are the "results and outcomes" of vocational skills and compatible assignments for actions taken. In context of this book, these results are produced by empowered and emotionally committed talent or teams in a supportive workplace environment.

A supportive environment refers to the structure of an organization. Established by the senior executive team, a workplace framework needs to establish and maintain cultural core values, inspire creativity and innovation, and bring about positive results that are measurable. The framework includes technical standards within the organization, how the "business of the business" operates, and the valuing, care, and development of people. A supportive environment is one where risk is rewarded; risks to create, innovate, and manifest positive results for the entire enterprise. Failure is not punished but rather used as a learning opportunity. Given that the workplace framework impacts virtually every area of an enterprise, touching or adjusting the framework should only be done at the most senior levels in an organization.

The definition I use to describe Industrial Age employee productivity is; "The doing of something that achieves in getting good results producing or resulting in something, especially in large amounts." This definition has been validated over and over again in the past 300 years as we made things with our hands and then machines. As we morphed into the Connected Age a more descriptive definition of employee productivity needs to be totally recast reflective of the worker, tools, workspace, and things produced.

While we still make things in the Connected Age the majority of productivity is now tied directly to technology in some way. Whether it be AI automation in manufacturing or populating sales leads from mining mega data repositories productivity has shifted significantly from a specific count to revenue producing results. This is the generation where we have witnessed individuals who with only one website or App became kazillionaires.

Connected Age productivity does not include a quantity or time; or use time as a measurement of a rate of production. Rather, productivity is measured in terms of objectively verified results and outcomes in a workplace where talent are vocationally aligned with their skill set, personality and temperament, and their assignments that best allow maximum engagement and play freedom. Technology may allow results and outcomes to be revealed in moments but the effort necessary before technology is involved to communicate, cooperate, collaborate, and co-create (C4) ideas into innovative realties may take some time. Efficiencies learned in play and mastery of the game at hand may reduce subsequent cycle times as individuals find their best productivity fit on teams before engaging their specific role.

In the workplace setting the two following questions describe and identify individual purpose. "Why am I and my engagement necessary?" And, "Why does it matter?" In the Industrial Age these questions were difficult if not impossible to answer as an individual. Individuals were not valued for who they were but rather their ability to repeat specific tasks to meet production quotas is what was valued. People in the Industrial Age workforce identified themselves as just being a number or like a machine, void of emotional integration with what they were doing. Purpose was thought of as just being a cog in the wheel of production.

The Connected Age reintroduced to a brand-new generation of emotionally integrated talent, Millennials, that work is just an extension of life. Their productivity in actuating outcomes individually and on teams validates their value and individual life purpose vocationally. Individual purpose is identified and validated thru proper productivity alignment and productive engagement. They are not just a cog on a wheel, but an integral member of a team of company talent that takes risks and actions to create

Productivity | Life Purpose and Drivers for Advancement

results that eventually achieve desired outcomes strived for. Their purpose is not to just push a button or sling a hammer. Their individual purpose is to use their intellect and instincts to create and innovate sustainable productivity gains individually and for their team that benefit not just their company but the global community as a whole.

The Industrial Age workplace with its productivity metrics and measurements limited productivity of the individual in order to maximize productivity of the position. In fact, it didn't matter the productivity potential of the individual as the productivity of the position was what was important.

Let me now introduce without comment the productivity drivers identified in literature and see what you think; keeping in mind results and outcomes. Productivity drivers include economic incentives, regular constructive feedback, recognition as individuals, adequate training, employee support when genuinely needed, expressing appreciative emotion, and senior level modeling of behavior.[106] Keeping employees focused on their job at hand; implementing employee loyalty programs through becoming a better manager, improving company culture, and maintaining neutrality; keeping employees happy through a wide variety of stress reducing and enjoyment increasing methods; being the boss people would like to work for; embracing and distributing technology and the cool tools technology provides; revising internal operations frequently to see where improvements are warranted; rethinking things to tweak often; and, reading between the lines to know what is not being said and openly addressing it.[107] Promoting work/life balance, listening and responding to company feedback, creating a company culture, rewarding behavior and recognizing special occasions, providing an outlet to vent frustrations, giving individuals responsibility to do things they want to do and providing guidance for how to do it, celebrating personal successes, and providing personalized scheduling for their needs.[108] Setting out live plants, having better space and furniture, providing exercise breaks, keeping promises, making managers happy, laughing, letting people use Facebook, starting a book club, encouraging sharing, and letting employees get on with their work.[109] Family care programs specifically designed to help develop strategies for kids, pets, and aging parents; flexible schedule work options for working at home or outside the office; taking breaks for birthday parties and celebrations that highly encourage movement, talking, and laughing; and demonstrating leadership in the form of regular employee appreciation recognition in the form of shout outs, publicity of accomplishments, and profiles in company literature.[110] Apple Store environment with abundant caffeine and cool web tech. Latest innovative technology, applications and personal proficiency. Encouraging parents to keep in loop with their kids' career. Annual performance reviews to explore organization career path. Build community internally and extend friendships beyond walls. Connect Millennial influencers with same in and out of company. Teach interpersonal skills for meeting and conversing with others. Invest time, energy, and emotion to see them succeed.[111]

Whew, and that was only a partial listing of what I found in the research for productivity drivers. Productivity is not driven by a perk, a back massage, or a smoothie bar at work.

All the perks were one thing, but now we are getting new infrastructure to enhance productivity. The following is a description of the new design elements of today's workspace; intriguing. Kathryn Hamilton describes the functionality and purpose of future office designing as follows: "While each entry showcased distinctive and abstract design elements, all of them incorporated universal themes of flexibility, practicality and personalization into creating unique spaces that increase employee productivity, function more efficiently and generate sustainability."[112] In a comment regarding the increasingly dynamic nature of commercial office trends to attract and retain top talent by catering to the employee experience rather than their career status, Thomas J. Bisacquino (CEO of NAIOP) says, "As progressive thought leaders in commercial real estate development, this year's winners have showcased exceptional cutting-edge, yet practical, concepts that will allow businesses to prosper as employees become more engaged from working in environments that nurture optimal performance."[113] Performance is tied directly to making those not too concerned about status very comfortable, and they are none other than Millennials.

The impact of a changing workspace was reiterated in a 2018 Forbes article entitled, "The Millennial Arrival And The Evolution Of The Modern Workplace."[114] In this article the authors noted, "Pampered and acclaimed, fussed over by recruiters, annunciated by the press, dissected by psychologists and analyzed by statisticians, the millennial generation

Productivity | Life Purpose and Drivers for Advancement

has fully come into its own, and that means big changes to the design and implementation of the modern workplace."[115] The big change includes trading out traditional office space itself for more flexible mixed and matched modular collaboration enhancing workspaces. "This evolution translates to workspaces, or activity-based working (ABW) models, that offer superior flexibility while allowing for the type of community-based collaboration that millennials find comfort, meaning and joy in."[116] The envisioned workspaces are more like lounges and break-out rooms. The biggest factor for allowing these AWB models has been the evolution of new technologies allowing greater flexibility and collaboration between users and devices.

A 2014 survey by the Millennial Branding Company was pointing to this when it identified the three most important ways Millennials preferred to work.[117] An almost unanimous ninety-eight percent of Millennial respondents wanted to be innovative and affecting change in the organization (very rare combination in Industrial Age business). Another majority of eighty-five percent wanted to be interacting with a diverse group including both coworkers and clients (again, not Industrial Age style). And finally, eighty-one percent of Millennials wanted autonomy (Industrial Age; hardly ever).[118] As they entered into the Industrial Age workplaces between 2008 and 2014, Millennials were sorely disappointed with what they found so many simply left. As Connected Age workplaces began to emerge in 2015, many Millennials began to find their groove in environments where relational comradery in creativity and innovation were engendered by peers and supervisors alike, and within companies where they were given the freedom to play, develop mastery, and be productive.

Industrial Age productivity was a cycle of make it sell it, make it again sell it again, until the product went out of style and you had to make something new and repeat the cycle. Each time you made a new product there was development, tooling, material expense, fabrication, distribution, over production and returns to deal with to name just a few cost centers. Time and expense to get products from conception to market was the safeguard against a rapid rise in competition or disruption. It was the Industrial Age safeguard; you had to already be in the business to be in the business. And if a competitor showed up, you'd have a sale during their launch, talk to their banker about a new mega-loan for your company, and then drive the competition in the ground. Then you'd have a few drinks and a laugh in the executive suite and go back to making it and selling it.

In the Connected Age of innovation and productivity, you can develop an App and put it on-line for $1.99. If you get 10,000 people in the first month to click on it to buy you probably have something; remember the Internet—a global marketplace with several billion people on-line. That first ten thousand will get you fifty thousand more sales the next month, one hundred fifty thousand more sales the next month, and by the sixth month your popping off one million sales per month and climbing. All you're paying for your is your internet connection, a passthrough to the App aggregator, a small coding team to keep updating the App, and a reputable CPA and lawyer to safely ferret away your cashflow. The biggest decision you have to make after eighteen months and twenty million users and rising is whether to sell the App for one hundred million cash or keep it and make six hundred million or more in the next three years. But in the back of your mind you know that on any given day a rival App could make your App obsolete, or a disruptor App or website could be introduced that would dramatically alter the entire App world. Either option would immediately end the gravy train. Sell now and pocket the cash; or take some reserves and build a new improved App; or get a partner and build the disrupter App yourself. So many great options, what's a person to do? WaHoo!

Compare that to Jeff Bazos, founder of Amazon in 1994 and now one of the world's richest person. His bookselling website, Amazon.com, his Internet fantasy business keeps growing larger every day taking over everything. You can be assured that the far majority of Millennials believe and work productively hard every day to either be, or be a part of, a Connected Age company. Bezos might have a head start, but Millennials likely have the Amazon disrupter almost finished and ready to roll out; The-Nile – Free Everything for one low monthly fee!

Millennials want a vocation where they can productively play all day and have leisure time to create and innovate. Millennial play is not in a childish sense of kickball but in a mature sense of intentionally experimenting with the edges of possibility; taking leisure time to consciously think and have "Aha" moments of inspiration of new ways of doing things; inventing useful things never seen before; and using

Productivity | Life Purpose and Drivers for Advancement

technology and AI to create a more sustainable planet. And they don't want to do it alone, but with a team of peers who have the same drive and passion from a wide variety of skill sets to envision, communicate, cooperate, collaborate, and co-create (C4) innovation. This is what they learned to do in school while we Boomers were busy working.

Millennial play at work is extremely productive because they're not working for retirement but want to create something special, real, beautiful, sustainable, and unique. Things are still missing that they will create to make their world better for everyone. They know in order to WIN a game they have to develop mastery in their area of expertise; i.e. complete functional knowledge. In order to WIN "games" they have to become an authority in their area of expertise; i.e. complete functional wisdom. As a subject matter authority, they would be able to create new better, faster, and more efficient ways of doing what they've spent years learning and doing.

Did I mention the millennium change cycle (MCC) tsunami that will be cresting around 2025? Think of all the tasks still done by hand at all the manufacturing, production facilities, and small businesses across the country. At one time those working hands were invaluable to getting products out the door. Millennials will automate those positions and begin to use the immeasurably more valuable minds controlling those same hands and allow those individuals to help co-create, envision, and innovate their business for the Connected Age.

Humanity has not changed since we were first created. We were specifically created in God's image to work, create, discover, and innovate. If you look back in time before the Industrial Revolution, we've done some pretty amazing things. And for the most part without any of the tools developed by our ancestors over the last 200 years. We've only just begun to be productive with the tools we now have. Unleash The Millennials to play with these tools and productively create and innovate their wildest imaginations with results and outcomes being the metric and measure. Get busy training Boomer and Xer talent to be coaches and let them be driven by their own passions to help your Millennial talent productively create and innovate results and outcomes that will actuate the millennium change they will bring about. Unleash The Millennials and Save the World.

Unleash The Millennials and Save the World

Chapter 15

Loyalty | Life Calling and Drivers for Work/Life Balance

The Industrial Age definition I use for employee loyalty is; "A person who works for another person or for a company and demonstrates complete and constant support with unwavering allegiance." This Industrial Age thinking is still common with the employer being in essence the master and the talent being just a resource or a tool.

I can't tell you how frustrating it is when my toolbox gets cluttered and I don't take care of my tools. Eventually I'll leave a screwdriver or wire snips somewhere random and when I need them, they are not where I needed them to be. As a result, I take one of several trips to the hardware store I'll make during any given project to find and buy a new screwdriver. If I'd just been more careful with my tools, I'd save a bunch of time and money.

The average time and cost of replacing an employee is somewhere around three months and between $15K to $25; a little bit more than a screwdriver. And wouldn't you know it when I'm done with my project, I have the new screwdriver in my hand and really don't want to rearrange my cluttered toolbox, so I open a drawer in a kitchen cabinet to temporarily store it. Then with a slap to my forehead I note the discovery of the once "lost" screwdriver and wire snips used on my last project. If you have trouble losing talent, look for where you were when you were done using them before they quit, and you may discover the resignation notices of the four prior employees that held that position as well.

Unleash The Millennials and Save the World

For the Connected Age, loyalty happens when talent feels a healthy emotional commitment to their workplace and are empowered and supported. In a work environment where there exists authenticity, shared values and purpose, integrity, and transparent communication, trust is possible. The result is employee loyalty—a strong allegiance to the company and people. All efforts benefit the company long term, as the talent sticks around.

Before we go through the loyalty drivers, I think it important to remind us all that work and life for a Millennial are all part of the same stream or continuum. Millennials are not compartmentally minded when it comes to life. As they become aligned over time and consistently/intentionally rebalance their engagement and productivity they will affirm their vocational calling. And if you implement the drivers of loyalty you may find yourself with a company filled with people who love the work they do and the company that provides them to opportunity to do the things they love.

The first driver of loyalty is healthy emotional commitment: Although this topic was addressed in detail in Chapter 13 on engagement, I'll add a short reminder comment. A healthy emotional commitment is one where Millennials recognize a part of their life is being engaged and productive in meaningful work at your company as affirmed by the company, their supervisor, and peers.

The second loyalty driver is a company culture of authenticity (i.e. genuine, real, actual, verifiable): Authenticity is the gateway that allows Millennials the freedom to be their true and best selves in every beautiful way. And they are beautiful in intellect, emotional integration, passion for meaning and purpose in life and for creativity and innovation in their vocation, and a desire to help those who may not otherwise be able to help themselves.

Authenticity is saying what you mean and doing what you say. Millennials are very astute and will mirror your authenticity or lack thereof. And by your own words and the validating actions that follow your Millennials will know whether their future loyalty to your company is profitable for them or not. If it doesn't matter to you than just admit it. Tell them plainly, "We'll explore authenticity one day; but for now, just do your job while we do ours." But do not expect authenticity from your Millennials or their loyalty.

Loyalty | Life Calling and Drivers for Work/Life Balance

Authenticity is not having a fake "family-like" culture promoted in literature and introduced at all client meetings and conference settings that current talent read, see, and hear and do not recognize. If executive leadership is unavailable or aloof, senior level leadership team driven to squeeze turnips for blood, managers unresponsive and lack empathy for the talent they supervise, and front-line talent afraid to mention how poor customer service is going than just admit it.

Now if employee engagement and productivity and how talent is respected and vocationally developed and moved into new positions as they advance are all spoken highly of by the company and yet no actual active programs are in place to do these things who knows that most of all? Be intentional and follow through with programs for development advancement, metrics and measurements, evaluations and assessments, and providing feedback.

In order to be authentic, you must be willing to be vulnerable to being found out, as well as vulnerable to the actions of others; it is both give and take. I remember hearing Ed Catmull, a co-founder of Pixar Animation and Disney Animation, in a conference presentation speak about a time when someone erased the "only" final edit of Toy Story 2 from their server. This was going to result in a several month delay and of course not be insignificant in terms of cost. But no one panicked or threw a fit. What they fortunately discovered as they were working on the fix was that one of the executives had made an unauthorized copy of the final edit on their laptop to take home for the weekend and review. Ed noted that while it was a pretty horrific discovery and a joyful recovery, there was no search for the culprit who erased the file to hang out to dry as an example to be made of those who do such things.

He said that in order to be creative and innovative you are going to have to take risks and accept the fact that risk means failures along the way; in-fact you should expect failures. It is another Industrial Age to Connected Age paradigm change to foster creativity and innovation by having supervisors not micromanage talent to prevent risk but rather making it safe for talent to take risks – that is vulnerability in action. Failures don't just demonstrate what doesn't work, but also illuminate critical things moving forward which would likely remain hidden had the failure not occurred. Specifically, in this case, how to ensure final edits are

Unleash The Millennials and Save the World

not susceptible to being erased and security of final edits to ensure unauthorized copies are not unknowingly taken off-site.

He made it a point to emphasize no one was in or got into trouble because of this event. Pixar's authentic culture of creative and innovative risks which talent believed, experienced, and became emotionally connected resulted in multiple box office animation successes and thirty Academy Awards.

Being authentic as a company is difficult as it has to start at the very top and be relentlessly upheld and pursued to fruition all the way to the underground parking personnel. This is a gut check for executive and C-Suite personnel who have to be willing to be willing to be vulnerable themselves with those they are empowered to lead. Vulnerability is not weakness but reflects courage to own, admit, and act according to your true self. People are very loyal to the courageous.

The third loyalty driver is shared values and purpose: Almost all Industrial Age companies went through self-examination exercises in the late 1980's and early 1990's at the beginning of the Technology Age. We discovered it was no longer acceptable to produce products and services that didn't always work or that were designed to fall apart soon after the warranty expired. The recession of the 1970's really had us get lean and as long as we had a captive market our customers would just have to make do with disappointment. And darn it, we may have made it a few more years if it wasn't for those awesome and inexpensive Japanese and Korean imports.

As our customers, and we also as customers, chased the less expensive and more reliable import glitter the revenue statements of our flagship corporations began to take a dive. If you can't beat them, out compete them became the mantra. But to be competitive we had to know what they knew; which of course they'd learned from one of us.

After World War II, one of our own, W. Edwards Deming, was sent to Japan to evaluate their postwar agricultural and production problems. Over a period of several years and trips to Japan, Deming in 1950 began to clue them in on several key metrics to measure and manage for quality control (QC) and constant process improvement. He was American so they listened and did what he said and the resultant impact of high quality and inexpensive imports over the next few decades on our economy was nothing short of devastating in many different sectors.

Loyalty | Life Calling and Drivers for Work/Life Balance

We decided to incorporate some of Deming's work in our corporations and another consultant showed up, Philip Crosby, who had the bright idea to "do it right the first time." For the next several years our companies from top to bottom went through either a Deming or Crosby program to develop Quality Assurance/Quality Control (QA/QC) systems, procedures, and cultures with the goal of zero defects and continuous improvement moving forward. It was at this time companies began developing Mission and Vision statements that would reflect to the world our organizations daily pursuit of purpose and hope for what our productive purpose would eventually actuate.

How soon the flower fades in the throes of a recession; which of course we had during the early 1990's. The training was stopped but many of the seeds planted before the hiatus continued. The most ubiquitous seed to flourish throughout the culture was the relatively easy to pen and post Mission and Vision statements. Many Industrial Age companies may still have Mission and Vision statements that have never been reviewed or looked at since they were put in the employee manual back in 1996. Come to think of it, many of these same smaller and closely held companies still haven't updated their employee manual since 1996; that's another subject but relevant just as well.

As the Technology Age grew into the short-lived Information Age it became evident that having a Mission and Vision statement weren't enough if you really had no metrics or measurements for what they were trying to reflect to the public and talent about "who" the company was culturally. In order to address this, it became common to publish values and/or core values that were to reflect in essence cultural competencies. We value quality, our customers, our people, etc. When the Connected Age finally emerged from the Information age the Mission and Vision purpose statements no one could remember, and our core values declarations began to bite back.

Millennials entering the workplace actually took the time before coming in for the interviews to read our Mission and Vision statements and our values someone from marketing had been posted in the "About Us" section of our website. Prospecting Millennials searched the web to discover our reputation and read reviews about us on aggregator sites. They had the audacity to compare what we published on the web to what others actually encountered when dealing with us. Once fully prepared for the interview they asked us with a straight face to explain our culture. Of course, we responded, "Who cares about our culture, I'm here to interview 'you' to see if 'we' want you to work for 'us!' I'm assuming you're here because you want a job?" The early literature on employer encounters with Millennials during interviews is replete with this type of exchange.

Soon it became known that Millennials did not as much think we were interviewing them for a job, but rather they were interviewing us to see if we were the type of company they wanted to work for. "Who gave them this right?" we asked. "We did!" is the answer. We thought it to our benefit to publish outdated and erroneous or irrelevant statements about who we were culturally because we needed something to put on our lobby wall and then moved onto our website. We didn't know what these materials said, much less cared because we were who we knew we were. Heck, everyone working here has been here since these things were first made up back in the mid-1990's and mid-2000's. We know who we are and what we do, and our customers know us as well; that's why we're still in business. Then we look around and realize most of the "we" just mentioned are no longer here. And who are all these new young people?

What we didn't know is that the Millennials have been taught to be skeptical of truth claims and have the tools, intellect, and desire to validate and be in agreement with where they will be spending significant "life" time. They expect to work in a place and in a position that have, surprising to many, morally and ethically strong guiding principles and values. And they expect that the purpose of the company they work for (i.e. our old school Mission and Vision) is one of employee care, customer satisfaction, sustainability of products and services, and a giving back in a philanthropic way a part of the profits their efforts have contributed to earning. Many Boomers may be scratching their heads and wondering, "And when do they expect we'll be making money?"

Here's the key word in regard to values and purpose, "shared." If you want to be in business after the millennium change cycle (MCC) tsunami crest, you'd better get this one right. After the tsunami crest most if not all customer purchasing managers will be Millennial. Not just the agent, but the managers of the agents. And they will realign their supply chain providers to those who have similar values and purpose to their own. Why buy from someone who is working contrary to your own companies' values and purpose? In order to figure out what those values and purposes

Loyalty | Life Calling and Drivers for Work/Life Balance

are going to be I strongly recommend immediately reevaluating values and purpose statements. Looking ahead to who will be employed within and running the organization in five years and the legacy of successful succession of Boomers out of the workplace. Take time with this one.

There is a whole lot of fomenting that spans two polar opposite extremes in our politically charged culture about values and purpose both for the individual and for companies and organizations. The good news is the extreme fringes, while vocal, are always a small minority when compared to the middle. Stay in the middle if that is where the customers are or on an extreme edge if likewise, the customer base is extreme. Just be consistent remembering Millennial sentiments reflect a desire to work in a company with strong ethical and moral values and meaningful purpose. Have key Millennials help with this and get it validated with an internal survey. And throw away those old outdated Mission and Vision posters hanging in your lobby.

The fourth loyalty driver is integrity (integrity parlays nicely with values and purpose just discussed). Think in terms of reputation between a company of integrity and a company void of integrity. Integrity refers to the strong moral principles (found in values) and moral uprightness in the exercise thereof. Think of values and purpose as the things said, valued, and done and integrity being their demonstration and validation.

Values and purpose are what people read, integrity is what they see and hear. Integrity would be to address talent or workplace issues with a genuine concern of making the situation right. If Millennial talent is valued make sure to train them for their positions and regularly provide them direct and honest feedback. They don't won't to hear "You're doing good." They want specific areas where their efforts are in comparison to expectations and how to improve. If the purpose is to provide customers sustainable solutions for their projects, regularly assess through metrics and measurements evidence of performance sustainability and evaluate with feedback both the customer and design and construction teams. This is where a good reputation is made and is critical to maintain.

Millennials want to work for the good guys. Those companies who when they share life with their family and friends, they are not ashamed to say where they work. In-fact, they'd rather not work than to have to work for a company with no demonstrated integrity.

Unleash The Millennials and Save the World

A simple Google search reveals a lot about an organization. If something is out there that is not reflective of reality talk about it openly, internally. Proactively address it internally, even if it is a misperception issue by a fringe observer. Demonstrate to Millennials on staff and to on-line detractors that listening is occurring and thoughtful responses rendered. Reputation is one of the number one reasons why a Millennial will not work for an organization, and they like to post their feelings on-line. Establish a company of integrity led by men and women of integrity who work alongside talent of integrity.

The fifth loyalty drive is transparent communication: This particular driver is another Industrial Age to Connected Age paradigm change of critical importance. Boomers were raised in a day where the telephone was affixed to a wall in the home or on a poll on the street. Innovation was when they put an extension cord on it, and you could put the phone on a counter; and did you say we could get one in a color other than black? Communication was when you spoke to someone on the telephone, or wrote something to someone by hand on paper, or else spoke to someone face to face. Communication in a business setting was utilitarian in that it was short and to the point. Need this, do this, deliver this, pay this, buy this, pretty simple.

Boomers have lived through the Age changes and we're enjoying the Connected Age toys but still communicating in Information Age utilitarian fashion. The problem with this is utilitarian communication is it is not fully effective on the other side of the business model paradigm change; in-fact it fails miserably. Communication in the Connected Age is to be transparent, i.e. filled with enough relevant information on the subject matter that it is "clear" what is being communicated and not open for misinterpretation. In a world where truth is very subjective, and communications open to one's own interpretation transparency (i.e. clarity) is imperative so as not to cause undue confusion or concern.

The mode, tenor, and actual words used in communication must be such that the originator and the receiver both understand what is being communicated. This typically requires the receiver to communicate back to the originator what they think they have heard so as to confirm they are on the same page. Differences can be quickly resolved, and the communication clarified.

Loyalty | Life Calling and Drivers for Work/Life Balance

Transparent communication with clarity feedback should be a routine and positive exchange between your talent and their supervisors and managers. This routine transparent communication with clarity feedback should continue up the line all the way the top executive in the organization. All business, even technology, is people business. People communicating with people transparently in the Connected Age makes for healthy workplace environments.

Transparent communication should allow any person to be able to communicate with any other person in an organization without ruffling any hierarchical feathers. This means that if a Millennial who is working on a design issue needs to speak with the head of marketing about something of common interest on his or her project there are not three levels of approval needed to get the two communicating. And likewise, if the head of finance needs to speak to a front-line Millennial in shipping to discuss ideas being considered to cut transportation costs, he or she doesn't have to go through two shift supervisors and a team leader to communicate.

In the Industrial Age you had to stay in your place in line, wait your turn, and earn a place at the table; that's just how things worked. In the old days the designer (i.e. the Millennial in the example) would have had to go to their supervisor and explain why they needed to speak to the director of marketing about their project. Their supervisor would either shoot the designer down right then or call the project director or department manager and they would discuss the designers request. They may conclude that the designer's reason for contacting the marketing director has no bearing on their project regardless of a common interest with marketing and the supervisor would relay the message, or not, back to the designer.

I have never liked standing in line. Being pretty confident of myself in the old days and often told by my supervisors to step back in line until I was called forward, I just kept my head down and mastered my craft. Finally, I grew tired of standing in line and opened my own company at age twenty-eight. By God's grace and favor work poured in the door sufficient to employ fifty-seven people in offices in three states four years later. Then I was made an offer to be acquired and became part of something much bigger in a public traded company. I accepted thinking of grander and greener pastures.

Unleash The Millennials and Save the World

I was appointed as a vice president division manager over my company's home office while my other two offices fell under different leadership within the acquiring company. Again, God's grace and favor poured in and starting with twenty-five people in four years we added a satellite office and grew to over 120 people in the division. We were the fastest growing and second most profitable office of over sixty offices globally. What I discovered over those four years was the grass was not greener and still need to be mowed, the lines to stand in to advance were much longer and harder to navigate, and turf battles at the regional level fractured any form of corporate team unity. So, I stepped out of the line and opened another company.

I think that one of the reasons I love Millennials so much is that they have no patience to stand in line to wait to do something they are entirely capable of doing on their own. They have been educated and trained to go directly to the best "source" and avoid intermediaries. Let them transparently communicate with whoever they need and allow them to just do their job.

Unless otherwise authorized and recognized as not for dissemination, transparent communication should be such that if it were openly shared with parties outside the formal to and from loop it would be recognized to be in full conformance with the stated company values and purpose. There is not "hide the ball" in transparent communication, us against them, dysfunctional behaviors, or withholding information. The importance of this in today's flash ready universally distributed social media panacea of speculations and cynicism, is that if something is communicated it is only a matter of time before it is made known to all in full view. Even President Trump's private conversations using the supposedly secure "bat-phone" with global leaders on his first day in the chair were leaked to the media that same day by someone listening in.

If there is something good happening somewhere in your organization, transparently communicate it appropriately internally and externally. Allow the entire organization and those who may visit your social media platforms in on the good news. This is not so everyone can get a trophy just for showing up, but should authentically represent continued wins for people, the company, and clients.

And finally, transparent communication must be consistently measured with objective metrics, evaluated, and feedback provided both

Loyalty | Life Calling and Drivers for Work/Life Balance

for positive results and failures. Remember, failures are to be expected so look for them. Not to render appropriate discipline but to authentically reward risk by correcting disconnect issues that improve the transparent communication process. The significance of consistency cannot be over emphasized. This is not a one and done effort, but as in all the drivers must become part of the fabric of the organization. The Industrial Age of utilitarian communication is forever dead. Get up to speed with Connected Age transparent communication and keep it going and Millennials will keep you going as well.

The sixth loyalty driver is trust. As consistency in loyalty drivers are rolled out, they will engender genuine trust not only from Millennials but also from staff of all generations. When individuals encounter an organization or person who is authentic in all circumstances, shares their same values and purpose, displays integrity, and whose communication has transparent clarity a genuine trust is imparted. This genuine trust is the loyalty bond glue for holding onto Millennials.

The best example of the disconnect of loyalty during the initial days of transformation from Industrial Age to Connected Age workplaces was revealed in a loyalty statistic of a very large 2013 HR manager survey mentioned earlier. The survey loyalty component indicated that eighty-two percent of Millennials responded they were loyal to their employers while only ONE percent of human resources personnel responded that Millennials were loyal to their employers.[119] This shocking differential revealed at the time that there was a real Millennial loyalty crisis in business. The Millennial turnover rate of a 2014 survey indicated that Millennial turnover was double that of older generations in the workplace.

By 2018, while many Industrial Age businesses were being replaced by Connected Age workplaces, the attitude of Millennials reported from large survey data revealed that ninety percent of Millennials indicated they were looking to grow their vocational careers within companies where currently employed. While the Millennial response to this particular survey was only eight percent higher than the 2013 survey previously mentioned (eighty-two percent being loyal to their employer) the respondents were gauging their loyalty on a career development stay and not just loyalty in general.[120] I believe this is reflective of both the current growing state of the economy and validation of the earlier survey that indicated Millennials are not transient by nature. However, when asked to engage and produce in an Industrial Age workplace they are more likely than previous generations to just continue looking for opportunities that fit them.

For completeness, the following is a continuous stream of loyalty drivers others have mentioned in literature I've reviewed. Communication, fairness, individual recognition, and meaningful rewards.[121] Quantification of employee engagement, solicitation of complaints, helping employees see big picture, using secret shoppers, closing training gaps, mentoring program, promoting team building, proactively addressing compensation complaints, telling the truth, getting rid of bad managers, and recognizing employee accomplishments.[122] Valuing people above all else, giving is getting (employee perks), trusting above all things, and ensuring employees know the significance of their work.[123] "Being valued and respected by one's employer is even more important in developing and maintaining loyalty than the company's work/family benefits."[124] Job satisfaction, relationships with managers and peers, salary, family considerations, and corporate benefits.[125] Measuring up against the competition so that the grass is just as green, talking with staff regularly to obtain and incorporate feedback, linking recognition to corporate values to educate about and reinforce the values, keeping recognition and incentive programs simple, continually and consistently selling the rewards and benefits of the incentive program.[126] Encouraging entrepreneurial passion and creativity, offering technological innovation, granting flexible-time options, and promoting giving back.[127] Pay, security, and career advancement.[128] A recognized company vision, having a career not a job, being part of something bigger, fair remuneration, feeling empowered, being challenged in a healthy way daily, proper training and development, recognition with relevant reward, strong management relationships, and work-life balance.[129] "Research shows employees who believe they are trusted by their managers and CEOs can better see the big picture and tend to be more loyal and productive, or in other words, more engaged."[130] "Employees who are offered substantive career development opportunities tend to be more engaged, and therefore more loyal and more productive."[131] "When people are treated as if they're important and truly make a difference, their loyalty and engagement soar."[132]

That's a pretty long list of loyalty drivers in addition to the ones I provided in the Connected Age definition. The intent of providing dump

Loyalty | Life Calling and Drivers for Work/Life Balance

listings of drivers is not to overwhelm but rather to summarize some of the myriad of articles written on Millennial engagement, productivity, and loyalty (EPL). Drivers included in the definitions herein for EPL were purposeful as they reflect the Best Practices I could discern from the literature. Of course, the top drivers ten years and counting for EPL are vocational development, career path advancement opportunities, and work/life balance. As you work with aligning talent in their engagement and productivity, provide them development, advancement opportunities, and work/life balance you will enjoy loyalty success. Unleash The Millennials and Save the World.

Unleash The Millennials and Save the World

Chapter 16

Boomer Paradigm | No Meaning, Purpose, and Calling

Before going on in the text I just want to introduce a few thoughts regarding the differences among life meaning, purpose, and loyalty in terms understood by Industrial Age Boomers vs. Connected Age Millennials. In a coaching session I was having with a Millennial we spent a lot of time hammering out what he envisioned gave his life meaning, defined his life purpose, and pointed to his vocational calling. Following the coaching session, as we were drinking coffee, he turned the table on me and asked about how I discovered my own life meaning, purpose, and calling when I was first starting out. I literally laughed out loud and then explained the life of a late twenty something Boomer around 1990. What I said was something similar to what I have below.

Boomers never learned or considered life meaning, purpose, or calling in their vocational pursuits. We were taught emotions and meaning were synonymous and were evolutionary artifacts of materialistic brain function that had not fully evolved. When people showed strong emotional responses, they were considered mentally ill and prescribed shock therapy, drugs, or a lobotomy in extreme cases. For Millennials reading this it may be horrifying to realize that advanced psychology and psychiatry during the era when Boomers were young really did involve hooking people's brains up to electrical currents trying to "shock" emotions out of them. If that didn't work, they'd prescribe heavy duty drugs to totally zone a person out for a season and then see how—or if— they recovered. If that didn't work, they performed a "transorbital" lobotomy which in essence was hammering a special surgical needle through an eye socket to scramble parts of the brain. People with scrambled brains didn't have emotional issues—or emotions— anymore. That was considered best practice in medical science! Boomers were conditioned not to be overly emotional. They kept problems within families, never honestly addressed ideas of happiness, loss, grief, loneliness, or inner fulfillment.

The Modern Philosophy and science of Boomers' youth did not consider the content of emotions to be knowledge. Knowledge was all part of something philosophy and science called prediction and control; if it can't be measured, it doesn't exist. If it doesn't exist, it is not knowledge and therefore it is not discussed or considered. Only what was physical and measurable was real. Thus, to deal with emotions, one simply denied them, or erased them with liberal amounts of alcohol or drugs.

When Boomers got old enough to work, they just did it. They did not question. Boomers had no sense that seeking meaning or purpose in work or life was worthwhile. We were taught work was part of the materialistic evolutionary human cycle, you are born, grow up, go to school, get a job, get married, have kids, buy a car and a house, retire, and die. If you happened to experience happiness or pleasure along the way—that was just a bonus. But don't be too happy or too sad as that may indicate emotional instability, and we all knew where that might lead.

Engagement in work meant doing your job well enough to keep it. If you had problems keeping a job, that was a slippery slope to emotional difficulty and Boomers wanted to avoid that. Some had to switch jobs several times until discovering something bearable they could do, and that over time allowed the other parts of the cycle to continue, ending eventually in death. For Boomers collectively, meaning and purpose were non-issues.

Think about it for a second. How much of what you do requires you to physically make something versus using your mind and technology to create text or images on a screen. Take that a bit further, how many of you, when you think of innovating something, think of a physical product versus a new technology or App? Industrial Age Boomers were not educated or trained to be productive in a technological environment. Now we adapted to it, with resistance at first, from the early to late 1980s, then we persisted, keeping up through about 2010. Finally, in a total rejection

Boomer Paradigm | No Meaning, Purpose, and Calling

of learning anything new, we hunkered down and have avoided new technology altogether. We'll learn what we have to in order to survive, but no more.

The truth is, we Boomers are tired of dealing with IT personnel and having to learn something new. We've been through about six full and all-encompassing technology learning cycles over the past forty years and are burned out. Boomers' first desktop computer in the early 1980's was likely an IBM model 5151 personal computer (PC) with twin floppy disk drives with a total memory capacity of a whopping 164KB. Combined, the floppy drives would barely hold a two-page PDF. Think about what we have had to adjust to technologically over the past fifty years.

Boomers have risen through the ranks only to discover all their technical and vocational skills left them ill-equipped to manage people, so we stopped trying. We're tired of dealing with people. Boomers have learned over the long haul that work would be great except you have to deal with people.

We're just holding on to retirement when we can cut off the cable, retire to a small home, replace the dreaded smart phone for a flip phone (no more emails!), get on Medicare while it lasts, and maybe collect Social Security checks, if they stop raising the minimum age to receive them. And darn-it, isn't that what we Boomers had kids for? To do all the new stuff and let the old geezers relax, except when it comes to spoiling the grandkids? (Boomers, you can laugh here…).

My Millennial client literally sat with his mouth open after my diatribe and said, "You're kidding me, right? You never thought about meaning or purpose, even today? That's all we think about!" I recommended he talk to his dad who is a few years older than I am to validate what I said.

At our next session he affirmed he spoke with his dad and now he really felt bad for us. He said something to the effect, "I think I'm really supposed to help you. Is there anything I can do to make you feel better?" I smiled and told him the best thing he could do was to seek, find, and live his life fully aligned with what gives his live meaning and purpose as he lives out his vocational calling. I also mentioned I was going to write a book (here it is a couple of years later) and he could buy a copy so I could at least have one sale. We both laughed out loud. Now I guess I'm going to miss that sale as I'll probably hand him a complimentary copy given he's made it into the book.

Unleash The Millennials and Save the World

The reason I am writing this is not to make Boomers suddenly freak out and think we have to get back on the horse and begin to figure out the latest technology, reinvigorate ourselves to manage people, or suddenly freak out that we never took time discover life meaning and purpose and validate our vocational calling. But rather be thankful for Millennials in our midst who were raised on technology, are people friendly, and have great plans to ensure awesome life meaning and purpose while they fulfill vocational callings that will literally save the world.

The significance of Millennial engagement, productivity, and loyalty has only begun to emerge and barely reveals what will be seen in the next three years to five years. I encourage my Boomer peers to embrace their last days in the workplace and intentionally reengage in their vocation thru coaching relationships with Millennials. They will take upon themselves all the technology challenges, allowing us Boomers to be a part of how far beyond Millennials will take what we started.

Have deep and engaging conversations with Millennials and love them just as you would your own children. Empower them in key areas of productivity, responsibility, and authority, and give them a long lead. Affirm for them that failure is not the end but the discovery of a lesson to be learned. Ask them to imagine the impossible and then give them the opportunity to prove themselves wrong. Millennials are not lazy; they've been burning the candle at both ends 24/7 since first grade. Give them a new candle and watch them light up the night!

Next, enjoy two short stories about engagement, productivity, and loyalty (EPL) and where fact and fantasy meet. The following chapter includes both an allegory about who Millennials are and what they are capable of doing if they are unleashed, as well as a true story involving the last vestiges of the Industrial Age mentality rubbing against the new Connected Age mentality. The first story is about sledgehammers and breaking rocks. The second story concerns those who read images of broken bones when people break things with sledgehammers. Unleash The Millennials and Save the World.

Chapter 17

EPL | Where Fact Meets Fantasy

Think of the great writers and artists of the past prior to the beginning of the Industrial Age (i.e. prior to 1600s) and identify for me their workplace engagement, productivity, and loyalty (EPL) drivers introduced by their employers that increased their contribution to the work. I'll present two individuals to consider and allow you to think of others, Saint Augustine, Bishop of Hippo (345 – 430 CE) and Leonardo da Vinci (1452 – 1519 CE). In case you don't know it, Augustine was a prolific writer and is considered to be one of history's greatest theological and philosophical scholars. He did not have a computer, electric light, air conditioning, or an endless supply of printer ink and paper. Yet the volume of written materials he produced was massive even by today's standards, and all of it is rich and replete with transcendent topics and concepts. His EPL was not a function of employer perks but a result of his engagement (meaning) in productively articulating his burning passion in writings (purpose), and never wavering from his loyalty to his God (calling).

Da Vinci is known as one of the world's most renowned artists even though only fifteen of his paintings have survived. He also spent vast brain power envisioning and designing innovations, including flying machines, solar power, and adding machines, while inventing many other practical machines for his day and our day as well. What were his employer perks that pushed him to create and innovate beyond what was already possible in his day and accepted as the norm? Why did he push beyond where many thought he was crazy for going? His productivity was not a

Unleash The Millennials and Save the World

function of employer perks but his own internal EPL drive unhindered by the restrictive thinking of his day.

Admittedly, not all Millennials are an Augustine or da Vinci but they are just as human with the same internal drive to discover life meaning (engagement), purpose (productivity), and calling (loyalty) in the life that they are living today and every day. The Industrial Age mentality in the workplace squashes all such thoughts of individuality and instructs us all to just pick up the sledgehammer and bang the rocks until they crack, pick up the smaller pieces and put them in the wheelbarrow, and repeat. After 300 years of this we all got pretty good at cracking rocks.

Then one day a Millennial showed up at work took one swing of the hammer, dropped it to the ground and walked away from the job. "The bum," we Boomers thought. "Too pampered by his mom to lift a sledgehammer and sweat a little. He probably expected us to crack his rocks for him and pay him double what we make because he then would think himself a supervisor." And we all laughed until the next Millennial showed up and did the same. Perhaps it was because the hammer was too heavy, and we didn't supply them with gloves. A lighter hammer and gloves did not prevent the next Millennial from walking off the job, although they did spend a full day hammering away.

Soon it was potted plants around the rock yard, portable air conditioners, rock and roll music played on awesome speakers, a smoothie bar with fresh and frozen fruit, matching tee-shirts with smiley faces that said, "We Crack-Up Together," cushy lounge areas for taking breaks, half-days off if quota was reached earlier in the week, and the pièce de résistance, a basketball court that had hoops with real nets. We finally thought we had it perfect. Millennials were at least breaking rocks with the rest of us, although they never did much beyond the minimum. The good thing to come out of all this was getting the perks we'd been demanding for years but that had never materialized until the Millennials showed up.

Then one day it was like someone turned off our sales line. Stash, our boss, called our biggest rock customer and asked if there was an issue with a shipment or order. "No," the customer retorted. "We've just contracted with a rock supplier that provides your same product for twenty percent of your cost."

EPL | Where Fact Meets Fantasy

"That's not possible," Stash responded, "let me speak to Jack in purchasing, he's been buying from us for years." The person on the other end of the line noted that Jack had retired, and Francis was the new purchasing manager. "Who's Francis?" Stash asked.

"She's a go-getter Millennial who is turning our business around," said the person on the other end.

"Well then let me speak to Francis."

Francis got on the line and was extremely polite and engaging and very empathetic with our situation, since we'd just lost our biggest customer. She explained that a new rock supplier opened up shop close to their location and had the capacity to support increasing demand at her facility, which was being expanded over the next few years. "And," she added at the end, "they supply rock at twenty percent of your price, with delivery." Stash asked who that supplier was, as they were likely a sham operation and would be out of business in weeks. She believed we were mistaken and suggested we check them out ourselves; SonicRok & Rol. Stash hung up as Francis was giving their web address.

A few of us jumped in the truck and motored over to this SonicRok & Rol to check out the losers who were so stupid to try and compete with us. We drove up and noticed the only entrance was through a guard gate. Aha, we had them, hiding behind a gate. We spoke to the guard who noticed our signage on our truck, Hammer-Time Rocks. "I know you," said the guard, "our CEO and founder Johnny said you were his first employer and he often uses Hammer-Time Rocks to inspire our workforce talent. I'll be right back," said the guard. He stepped away from the window, placed a call, and returned with a smile. "Johnny is so glad you are here and asks that you meet him at the welcome center. Take a left at the stop sign and the welcome center is straight ahead."

When we got to the welcome center, we saw a young, professional looking thirty-something standing on the porch awaiting our arrival. He walked out to greet us. As we were getting out of the truck, he greeted us each by name, "George, Pete, Stash, you are my inspiration and the result is all that is around you." As we gazed the horizon, we initially didn't see much beyond a huge rock pile and a massive metal building. It was Stash who pointed to a fleet of delivery trucks being loaded in an area on the opposite side of the facility. Yet there was no noise, no clouds of rock dust in the air. This did not make sense.

Unleash The Millennials and Save the World

We were all still gawking at our surroundings as Johnny led us inside to a massive, beautiful, open exhibit room covered on every surface with masterfully hewn stone of nearly every variety and color, all polished to perfection. Johnny directed us to a seating area on the left side of the room and we each took a chair. The seating area was the only thing in the immense room. "If you'd like something to drink," Johnny noted, "just open the right armchair cover and select what you'd like and leave the cover open." He then demonstrated by opening the arm cover on his chair, pressing a few times on a touch screen pad, and within seconds a bottle of mineral water emerged from the arm rest. Befuddled, we all did the same, only Pete knocked his bottle from the holder as he tried to grab it.

Although the real glass bottle fell on the stone floor, it didn't break. "Happens all the time," Johnny quipped, "I've even done it myself recently. We need to get that fixed. We already fixed the breaking glass issue with our supplier. You can drop that bottle from three stories up and it bounces about three feet high. Funniest thing you'd ever see or expect. But it works."

I started the real conversation by explaining to Johnny our call with our old customer and our concern about his pricing being unrealistic and unsustainable. Johnny assured us his pricing was good and that he was making a very comfortable living at those prices. "Have you looked around?" he asked. "This stuff isn't free." And then Johnny politely reminded us that it was no longer our customer but his or the next competitor that beats his price. It was Stash who went next and zeroed in on the issue.

Stash said, "I've figured it out; it took me a while, but I now know who you are and what you're doing."

"Go on," Johnny said.

"You're Jonathon, the first Millennial we ever hired, and you didn't last past one swing of the hammer. When you walked off the job, we thought you were just a loser. I'm just being honest. But you are no loser. I don't know what you did next, but I know you're now using a third generation Zeno or similar sonic blaster to break the rock in an enclosed environment much smaller than your metal and acoustically equipped dampening building. As pieces of the rocks reach specified design sizes they are captured on sieves and transferred into cyclone scrubbers

EPL | Where Fact Meets Fantasy

somewhere else in your building. As the rocks are cleaned of dust and impurities, they are conveyed underground to the loading dock at the other side of the facility. Your capacity could be anywhere from 100 to 500 times ours with an operating net revenue of about fifteen percent at your prices." Johnny smiled and only said, "You're a little low on the capacity and you'd only cry if I told you how low on the net revenue."

Pete had had enough and simply got up and walked to the door. Stash and I were still looking at each other when Pete asked, "Aren't you coming?" As we got to the door, Johnny stood up and asked Stash to wait just a minute as he had a question he'd like to get answered. After a few minutes, Stash walked up to the truck and motioned for me to roll down my window; which I did. "Sorry guys," Stash said, "I'm not going back with you."

"Why? What happened?" I asked.

Stash continued. "After you left, Johnny asked me to retake my seat as he wanted to show me something. He pulled out his cell phone and launched an app. As the lights began to dim the entire room became illuminated in a 3D hologram of the entire facility. I'm not talking about a picture but a live image of the facility including seeing you both get into the truck. Johnny had an innovation he was working on but was stuck and needed someone with vision and experience to take the lead. Not telling me what it was, he just said if I stayed with him today, allowed him to give me a tour of the facility, and sit down with their innovation catalyst coach for a couple of hours, he would appreciate it."

"Did he offer you a job?" Pete asked.

"No, he just said that there was an opportunity for a visionary and innovator within his company. And if I really thought in my heart of hearts that my meaning, purpose, and calling involved actuating innovations that I should stick around. If I was leaning that way but not sure, I should stick around. But if I didn't think that matched who I was or what I wanted to do, that I should just get back in the truck. And at the end of the day if I stayed, no matter my decision, he would have his driver give me a ride back to our facility. He then asked if he and his wife could take Sonya and I out to Spencer's for a steak dinner as thanks for my time spent answering my own curiosity. Sorry fellas," said Stash, "I've got a tour to take and I'm eager to get started earning that steak dinner."

Unleash The Millennials and Save the World

You may be wondering why I just had you read all that which was likely the same kind of wondering Pete and George chewed on all the way back to their facility. Of course, in addition to wondering, they agreed it was time to give everyone a two-week notice, freeze all purchases, close all accounts, and pull out whatever money they could before the bank came calling on the loan payments they owe for all the perks strewn across the workplace area. This is an example of the millennium change cycle (MCC) tsunami crest I've been speaking about.

In this example, Johnny had the passion for selling rock. What he couldn't figure out was why cracked rock which was relatively plentiful and distributed across the globe was so expensive. Johnny had seen an ad for an opening at Hammer-Time Rock and jumped at the opportunity to figure it out. And it only took him one swing of the hammer to answer his question – labor to break and segregate rock. It took him less than thirty minutes to find Zeno Sonic on the Internet and discover their third-generation machine used in underground tunneling. He called the company and asked about breaking rock with their machine above ground. The salesman said they had no machine for above ground application. Johnny asked to speak with their corporate innovation coach.

From the coach Johnny got Julius's name and number, a new Millennial they just hired in R&D. Johnny called Julius and explained what he wanted to do. Julius asked for a couple of weeks and he'd get back to him. In two weeks, Julius asked Johnny to sign a non-disclosure agreement he was sending him and then arranged, through their HR department, a flight and hotel for a meeting at their corporate office the following week. Johnny showed up and met with Julius and his team. They showed Johnny their plans for an above ground rock breaker but had lots of issues yet to work out. After a few more meetings, Johnny convinced them to license their technology to him and fund his design for construction of an operational facility to test and prove the concept which he would own, returning to them half the profits for ten years or until they recoup their investment twenty times over, whichever comes first. The deal was signed and that's what happened, in this mythic tale of Millennial ingenuity.

Now for a true story about the current interface between Industrial Age and Connected Age workers in the same profession—in this case, radiology. Julie and Samantha are radiologists. Julie is a Boomer in her upper fifties and Samantha is a Millennial in her early thirties, just finishing her residency program. Like most Boomers, Julie has spent her entire career in a seemingly continuous cycle of learning new and improved imaging technologies and systems to use in her practice. With each iteration, the imaging improved dramatically and the volume of data from the imaging increased almost exponentially.

Recently Julie has had to learn a behemoth of a new and vastly improved imaging system and the related instrumentation. Think of manipulating and viewing cloudy black and white X-ray images clipped to a light board versus 3D full spectral color spatial holography. Or working with an Excel workbook vs. an Oracle meta-data repository. She's been burning her nearly spent candle at both ends learning the new system and is dog tired. It is not optional. Her continued practice in the field requires mastery of the new system. She does part of her work the old way and, increasingly, part of it on the new system. She's really looking forward to retirement and regaining control of her life.

Samantha, as a radiology resident at a teaching hospital, has been learning on the new system and thinks it is fantastic. She cannot imagine radiology in the past without the level of detail now available. She may have a vague idea that the field used to involve a lot of guessing and intuition based upon experience. She's happy that the current technology allows the level of detail that educated guessing is nearly eliminated and intuition is focused on solutions and not the original problem. She's even more excited about what's coming next as it promises to make the imaging even more exacting and fast.

Now arises the issue between the Industrial Age and Connected Age productivity drivers the MCC tsunami will settle. Julie has heard the next iteration of imaging will include AI that will actually read the image and produce reports of findings within seconds. Julie thinks this is the craziest thing she's ever heard. Reading and interpreting images is how Julie makes a living! Now her future looks like reading and interpreting AI produced imaging reports. Julie knows an automated AI imaging system would not eliminate her practice but significantly take a bite out of her income. Her hope is to make it to retirement before such a system comes on-line.

Samantha on the other hand is super excited about AI interpreted imaging and reporting. It cuts out a lot of the busy work to get to the answers. Just think how much more she could get done in a day if she and her peers weren't spending most of their hours reading images but rather interpreting reports with the imagery to discern accuracy of the reporting. As far as income due to this AI advancement, Samantha thinks it is reasonable to assume incomes will remain the same or increase due to the volume of work one team of radiologists can do with the new system. She got into medicine to help people, and it makes sense to help more people with the latest technological advances.

Samantha would say, for example, "I am able to discern through imaging that the patient has an issue that, if addressed immediately, will result in a normal lifespan. If the procedure is delayed, the patient will die. How much is that particular life or death information worth? If the life or death scenario were dependent upon the imaging interpretation, doesn't it make sense for AI to read and interpret the image in seconds and create a report. With AI critical alert capability my team would be immediately notified of the findings so we could quickly review and confirm? Without AI, we may or may not be immediately available when prompt reading and interpretation of the image is vital. Thus, the patient's life is at risk."

The point of the Hammer-Time Rock vs. SonicRok and Rol story and the real-life account of Julie and Samantha is both illuminate who Millennials really are! They are not lazy, void of originality, only thinking about personal time. They are energized by the Connected Age electricity pulsing through their veins trying to do what they need to do—to pursue with passion their purpose. Productivity is not a unit-over-time thing for them. It is innovative results and outcomes that matter.

As mentioned in the previous chapters, empowering and inspiring individuals of all generations to discover their own best ways for creating desired results and outcomes is through coaching. In the next chapter we'll briefly explore an EPL coaching program I developed specifically to actuate Millennials to be optimally creative and innovative in the workplace; to run loose and play with all their might. Unleash The Millennials and Save the World.

Chapter 18

EPL Coaching | Gateway to Creativity and Innovation

There are many Millennials in workplaces today who feel overlooked and unappreciated for who they are and what they are capable of doing. They are thinking: What am I doing in this job? How am I to do my assignment? How is what I do related to everything else in the organization? Who decided it was to be done this way? Does anyone here really know what is going-on or care? Is there a career path in what I do or is this a dead-end job? Does anyone know that I actually know something? What is the next step beyond this position? How far can I go up and how fast? What lateral career path moves are available? How long do I suffer before I get work/life balance? How do I find a job that I love?

This thinking is not self-contained but spreads to talent feeling misunderstood, underutilized, undervalued, unsupported, underwhelmed, ignored, isolated, lonely, disconnected, and disrespected by the internal community of those with the keys to institutional knowledge. They become frustrated with having to wait in line and downcast because of cynicism and misrepresentations of character by older generations. Eventually exasperation sets-in with not being allowed to do what they know to do.

In response, they do the best they can under sometimes difficult workplace environments. Often, they find feedback non-existent and search for an outlet to gain perspective with peers in outside organizations. All the while they are surfing social media that post career path positions to look for better opportunities.

Unleash The Millennials and Save the World

The engagement, productivity, and loyalty (EPL) Coaching program presented herein was specifically designed to counter this Millennial thinking, feeling, and doing. Rather than having lines to stand-in, EPL Coaching uses specific research-based methods for empowering, enhancing, and actuating positive play, mastery, and discovery for creativity and innovation in the workplace as described below:

> **Empowering** alignment, development, advancement along individual career paths while optimizing work/life balance.
>
> **Enhancing** workplace engagement, productivity, and loyalty.
>
> **Actuating** creativity and innovation using the best in coaching techniques and EPL drivers.

The coaching program uses essential language, empowerment, and alignment as the framework to provide talent with the analytical and verbal tools needed to transparently communicate, cooperate, collaborate, and co-create. Each vocational position in the myriad of business sector possibilities has many unique metrics and measurements for assessing EPL. In order to simplify and be as generic as possible, the EPL Coaching program I present herein uses as the main metrics of measurement talent-experiences of subjective emotional based criteria. These particular metrics of measurement are universally applicable in all business sectors and very helpful in actuating the ultimate purpose of EPL Coaching which is for talent to discover for themselves life meaning, individual purpose, and affirmation of vocational calling.

Once established, the coaching program framework allows articulation of most logical and desirable career paths aligned with meaningful engagement, purposeful productivity, and loyal practice of their vocational calling. This involves a big serving of healthy emotional commitment of talent who want to achieve what they strive for on their own terms in a workplace where they feel valued. One of the many positive outcomes of EPL Coaching is enhanced talent creativity, innovation, and balance in all areas of work and life.

EPL Coaching works for everyone, regardless of their generation. For the Industrial Age Boomers who see doing tasks that produce outcomes to achieve goals as the way things should work, EPL Coaching fits the bill. In the EPL Coaching model Boomers identify and articulate the goal(s) and outcomes they hope to achieve, how to measure success, and the steps to be taken to get there. The coach and Boomer then establish metrics that can be tracked along the path to achieving their goals. EPL success occurs in harmony with sustained assessment, evaluation, challenges, and support

For the Connected Age Millennial, coach and talent begin by designing EPL games that will develop mastery. The goal of this coaching is seen thru the lens of masterful productivity. As the Millennial plays EPL games for achieving mastery they will discover along the way new heights of vocational development. Development leads to creativity and innovation and clears multiple paths toward advancement opportunities.

Not everyone wants vocational development. That is to be expected and respected. But for those who want development and can commit, there is a price to pay. Talent must be actively involved in the process, taking the actions they identify as their best way to overcome challenges and create their desired results. This is an important emotional commitment to accept and embrace empowerment for achieving their own career vision. Constant attention to practicing skills that increase confidence in taking actions cannot be emphasized enough in terms of producing desired results.

As described more fully in an earlier chapter, coaching has been identified by multiple research-based studies to be best practices in the delivery and reception of workplace learning content. Coaching is an authentic relationship between coach and client that engages the innermost part of the client and orients their language, empowerment, and alignment of thinking and behavior with their truest motivation/driven desires.

Millennials thrive in a coaching environment as it naturally fits with how they were educated. They have been educated and trained to be curious and play with problems for the enjoyment of learning, master their play with others for creatively innovating desired results, and discover outcome actuation from actions taken.

The culture of the traditional Industrial Age workplace is not prepared to effectively use the unique skill sets of Millennial talent. These unique skills are associated with the Connected Age pedagogy with which

Unleash The Millennials and Save the World

Millennials were raised and educated. Coaching provides the perfect tools and methods to bridge generational and cultural gaps among Millennials and older generations in the workplace.

Mentoring and/or apprenticeship were considered best practices and mainstay ways of training vocational and technical skills in the Industrial Age. We made things with our hands and used our minds on how best to direct them. Whether it was to guide a horse, swing a hammer, work a lathe, write a contract, or build a bridge of stone and wood. As the Industrial Age expanded, population centers developed, and resources increased we moved to public education of the masses.

Education once taught in small groups of multiple ages and subjects became age level, single subject, with students sitting in rows and columns. The teacher became the subject matter expert and students were conditioned to learn what they were taught and do as they were told. Does this sound familiar to anyone in the workplace? This type of thinking and instruction for Industrial Age learning is the round hole in today's Connect Age square peg workforce.

The Industrial Age paradigm for learning and achievement can be described by the following progression. This progression is engrained in the minds of most if not all Boomers in the workplace.

Task Oriented – Do this to make widget, then repeat...

Outcome Based – Make more widgets today than yesterday...

Goal Focused – Become largest widget producer...

Today's workforce was educated from secondary school through college to occupy jobs and career paths that had not been invented. While there is a resurgence of a desire to make things, this activity as well as almost every other business endeavor will be guided by the development and use of new knowledge. This new knowledge is mined from meta data repositories that store all the worlds digital based information, updated daily. We are only now in 2020 beginning to see the implications of having access to and manipulation, assimilation, and synthesis of knowledge contained in myriad meta data mines of the Connected Age.

EPL Coaching | Gateway to Creativity and Innovation

In order to prepare students for unknown vocational futures that would involve technology Millennial students were taught to work cooperatively in small group or pods and play with knowledge using multiple subjects weaved into the lessons (i.e. STEM and STEAM). Assignments once done by a single student were assigned to groups and the assignment broken into pieces. Searches of global knowledge available on the Internet were made for each piece and assimilated by the team into a final report.

There was not a predetermined result expected by the instructor for the assignment but rather a hope for a "discovery" of something entirely new. And more often than not, the sum of the parts was of much greater value than the pieces alone. Not only were the final work products of the group more robust than a single person effort, completion of the report took only a fraction of the time required for a single person to complete.

Today's workforce is now being asked to use that same process and machine learning algorithms of artificial intelligence (AI) to create who knows what. Millennials are on the front-line of this reality.

The Connected Age paradigm for learning and achievement can be described by the following progression. This progression is engrained in the minds of most if not all Millennials in the workplace.

Play Oriented – Play with knowledge to find its importance...

Mastery Based – Assimilate and synthesize knowledge...

Discover Focused – Creatively innovate "new" knowledge...

Presented below is a brief outline of an example EPL Coaching program with seven one-hour Modules designed to be conducted during lunch hour coaching sessions. This outline is not a one and done cookie cutter coaching program but is open for modification and tweaking to best fit the organization and workplace.

Unleash The Millennials and Save the World

EPL Coaching Program Outline
Modules 1 to 7

Module 1: Innovation Catalyst Coaching – Coaching Process, EPL Coaching Program
   What is coaching and why it works
   Metrics and measurements (M&M) for evaluating EPL
   Expectations, Commitments, Assignments
   Starting Baseline Coaching Assessment

Module 2: Essential Language – Trust, Truth, Honesty, Integrity, Keeping a Confidence
   Motivation expectations defined for each term by talent in workplace framework
   Communicate, cooperate, collaborate, co-create Essential Language in workplace

Module 3: Alignment – Personality/Temperament (P/T) vs. Position and Assignment
   Using assessment tools to evaluate talent P/T in regard to position and assignment
   Find right fit for talent in their "comfort zone" empowerment area(s)
   Communicate, cooperate, collaborate, co-create Alignment in framework

Module 4: Engagement – Optimizing Talent Empowerment in Framework
   Defining talent and workplace framework for meaningful engagement
   Identifying engagement strengths, weaknesses, misalignments
   Communicate, cooperate, collaborate, co-create Engagement in framework

Module 5: Productivity – Optimizing Talent Productivity in Framework
   Defining talent and workplace framework for purposeful productivity
   Identifying productivity strengths, weaknesses, misalignments
   Communicate, cooperate, collaborate, co-create Productivity in framework

Module 6: Loyalty – Optimizing Talent Loyalty in Framework
   Defining talent and workplace framework for loyal vocational sustainability
   Identifying career development and advancement opportunities
   Communicate, cooperate, collaborate, co-create Loyalty in framework

Module 7: Sustainability – Metrics & Measurements (M&M)
   Defining regular talent and framework M&M and scheduling evaluations
   Communicate, cooperate, collaborate, co-create sustainable M&M within framework
   New Baseline Coaching Assessment and complete End of Program Survey

Initiating an EPL coaching program begins with identifying internal coaches and Millennial (and Xer) talent to be coached. A workplace coach is an individual who has a bit more experience vocationally and sufficient company tenure to know where the holes are located. He or she does not have to work in same group or even be in your same business line. They can even be a peer. Two main characteristics you want to look for in a coach are integrity and demonstrated willingness to give straight constructive feedback.

EPL Coaching | Gateway to Creativity and Innovation

Selecting a workplace coach is the beginning of a relationship that involves open and transparent communication. And because this is a relationship and involves time, not all potential coaches have the desire or time to commit to being be a coach. You may have to go through a few invitation iterations to find those who have the passion for coaching that matches their qualifications.

Once selected and over time with transparent conversations, coaches will learn what gives and saps talent energy. The role of the coach is NOT to tell talent what to do. Rather, coaches use engaging questions to help talent articulate what they need to keep doing to keep moving forward. And coaches are there to celebrate successes.

Millennial talent participating in the EPL Coaching program should be personally invited by an executive leader. The invitation would be to consider participating in the EPL Coaching program designed to enhance creativity and innovation. With the invitation include a written document describing the coaching program, roles, responsibilities, and participation expectations for active engagement of empowerment for their own development enhancing their own career path advancement.

Module 1 – Innovation Catalyst Coaching

The first module is where program materials are handed out and discussed. Coaches and participants go over the coaching process and an overview of the next six modules. Discussions on metrics and measurements of subjective emotional based criteria and happiness, EPL Coaching expectations, and participant commitments are followed by completion of a Baseline Coaching Assessment.

One of the important expectations discussed is the need for coached talent to discuss with their supervisors their coaching commitments; what they have agreed to accomplish and the time frame. While supervisors may not be coaches, the purpose of the meeting is for supervisors to ask coaching type "constructive" questions about what they should expect to see different from the talent moving forward.

Answering direct questions from supervisors allows talent to hear and consider their own articulated responses/answers to questions they may not have considered in their coaching session. There are no right or wrong answers to questions, but rather opportunities for insight and revelation.

Unleash The Millennials and Save the World

Supervisors may be the most influential person in identifying talent development opportunities and consideration for advancement. Think about what it would mean to articulate, in response to supervisor questions, positive and constructive thoughts about a desired career path and advancement opportunities. Then think about the opportunity supervisors would have to fill advancement opportunities within the company with someone he or she recognizes as a perfect fit from their group. WIN-WIN.

Not all relationships last and the same goes for coaching relationships. If the relationship is not working, myriads of reasons, graciously end the relationship and find another coach.

The process of EPL Coaching is modular and cyclical. While the cycles can be entered at any point it is best begin with the first module which we are discussing now. The abbreviated cycle is align, develop, advance. The full coaching cycle, see graphic below, is baseline coaching, align, engage, develop, produce, and advance. Repeat cycle after each advancement.

Central to the EPL Coaching cycle for Millennials is optimizing Work/Life balance at each step along a career path. Work/Life balance Millennial talent is looking for is shown in the following table.

EPL Coaching | Gateway to Creativity and Innovation

Optimal Work/Life Balance Motivations	
Work	Life
Love What I Do	Do What I Love
Pursue a Life Giving Career	Lead a Fulfilling Life
Be Present & Well Rested	Be Present & Well Rested

Baseline Coaching is a self-completed assessment that addresses key areas for talent to envision their career path. Presented below is a Baseline Coaching Assessment I use in my coaching practice.

BASELINE COACHING ASSESSMENT | EPL COACHING

PURPOSE
1) Empower Talent to Align, Develop, Advance along Career Path.
2) Enhance Engagement, Productivity, and Loyalty in workplace.
On 1-10 scale Rate your desire to actuate this Purpose: ___
On 1-10 scale Rate your confidence to actuate this Purpose: ___

CORE VALUES
Identify three to five Core Values motivating you to wake-up and do something positive in your Work/Life.

PRESENT ASSIGNMENT
Provide responses for each item below. Leave blank if no answer.
    1. Your Vocation: 2. Position/Assignment:
    3. Required Education: 4. Required Experience:
    5. Career Path: Yes or No   6. Continue or Change Path

ADVANCEMENT OPPORTUNITIES
For YOUR career path identify below next known advancement opportunities and development needed to advance. Limit time horizon to three years. Leave blank if not applicable.
    1. Unfilled position(s):   Development:
    2. Succession opening(s):   Development:
    3. To be Vacated position(s):   Development:
    4. Expansion opening(s) due to Growth: Development:
    5. New Dept & New Office opening(s):   Development:

Unleash The Millennials and Save the World

DEVELOPMENT GUIDES
Identify by name Guides who can help you navigate career path Development and Advancement within your organization. If possible, identify a person for each organizational area listed.
    1. Administrator/Support:
    2. Human Resources:
    3. Supervisor:
    4. Department Manager:
    5. Vice President:
    6. Executive Team:

TECHNICAL OR MANAGEMENT TRACK
There is a fork in almost all career paths: 1) Continuing to develop technical mastery with a result of eventually leading a technical group; or 2) While maintaining technical acumen, focusing on management issues in order to foster future organizational leadership opportunities. Both roads beyond the fork involve leading people/teams. The first road focuses on doing the work and the second road focuses on managing the business in which work is being done. Which road would you choose?

    1. Technical Path _____   2. Management Path _____

WORK/LIFE BALANCE
Finding optimal Work/Life balance is a moving target depending upon many factors including career path mastery and loyalty to a vocation and/or a company. Identify for your current position and your next known advancement opportunity what you consider reasonable expectations of an optimal Work/Life balance.
    1. Current Position:
    2. Known Advancement Opportunity:

OPPORTUNITIES of FOCUS
Using YOUR Advancement Opportunities listing, identify primary and secondary opportunities that best fit YOUR individual career path and track option (technical vs. management).
    1. Primary Advancement Opportunity:
    2. Secondary Advancement Opportunity:

EPL Coaching | Gateway to Creativity and Innovation

GUIDES
Using YOUR Development Guides listing, identify Guides by name for both your primary and secondary advancement opportunity. These Guides must agree to help you select and obtain appropriate Development and be willing to openly identify YOUR areas of deficiency not easily fixed by experience and/or education.
    Guide 1:
    Guide 2:

GAME BOARD & RULES
Complete/edit/modify Game Board fields daily if possible, and no less than weekly. Failure to use a Game Board will likely result in stagnation along career path. Play your Career Path game to WIN!

Game Board Results
Identify at least ONE to THREE achievable Results within the next few months to best prepare for applying and being considered a qualified candidate for desired advancement opportunity.

Game Board Actions
Identify at least ONE to THREE Actions that can be taken today or this week to create desired Results.

Game Board Challenges
What known Challenges will prevent you from taking identified Actions today or this week to create Results?

Game Board Evaluation
What objective metrics & measurements will you use to evaluate success and identify challenge areas?

Game Board Skills
What skills need improving to overcome Challenges, to take better Actions, to create better Results?

MEANING of WINNING
Write a brief statement of what it would "mean" to you personally if you were EMPOWERED to Align, Develop, and Advance in your career path (and you did) and you Enhanced your Engagement, Productivity, and Loyalty in the workplace (and it showed).
                  End Example Baseline Coaching Assessment

Unleash The Millennials and Save the World

A Baseline Coaching assessment should be conducted immediately following every career path advancement. The reason for the assessment is to reset all the coaching parameters and envision career path progress toward the next advancement opportunity.

It is during the Coaching process where career path aspirational thoughts clash with desired work/life balance parameters. Baseline Coaching assessments help to straighten out tight and dead-end curves in the career path and open the way to a long and fulfilling vocational career.

Using the Baseline Coaching assessment as a guide, the next parts of the cycle include alignment for succession or growth opportunities; engagement in empowered duties; development by key IK holders in areas of critical need; productivity in empowered areas; and advancement along technical or management tracks. Rarely are career paths straight lines and often divergences are beneficial to reaching the final goal. The important thing is that whatever is done or pursued is done so with intentionality so that desired outcomes fall in-line with the coaching plan.

Life is not predictable and often involves huge and unanticipated challenges. As a result, career paths can at times be difficult to predict well in advance. However, lack of predictability is not a reason not to plan and prepare for success. Use the cycle to your advantage and envision, align, develop, and advance often

Module 2 – Essential Language

This is the key one-hour module for success in the remainder of the program. And even if there were no modules after this one, what talent get out of Module 2 can last an entire career. This module presents the path to transcendent truth and knowability and into the world of creativity and workplace innovation. The purpose of Module 2 is to have the employee articulate his or her own definition and metrics for trust, truth, honesty, integrity, and keeping a confidence. Next, we repeat that process to discover how that works on the job—in other words, what the company and the employee's supervisor would expect. All these terms are interwoven with each other and are imperative for actual "learning" of true and knowable things in the workplace.

Clear, transparent, well defined and agreed upon essential language is THE workplace essential for creativity and innovation. I suggest using

EPL Coaching | Gateway to Creativity and Innovation

four key words and a phrase to establish the baseline for all essential language used in the workplace. Upon this baseline, workplace values need to be fully articulated, understood, and agreed upon by all parties. Only in this way can true cultural expectations be experienced enterprise wide and amplified in all communication, cooperation, collaboration, and co-creation (C4) both internally and externally.

Using whatever resources and/or references necessary, talent is to define as objectively as possible the following four words and phrase: Trust, Truth, Honesty, Integrity, and to Keep a Confidence (i.e. to keep a secret). Once defined, the talent is to request their direct supervisor to define the same.

Following definition by both talent and supervisor they are to meet and agree upon a common definition that aligns with the expectation of workplace framework and put into writing. In other words, the definition of language locally should not diverge widely from what would be expected by company talent while on the job.

Each of these words are interrelated, and thus dependent upon one another. A failure of meeting the definition for one may also mean failure in meeting the definition for the others. This definition exercise, discussion with supervisor, and mutual agreement of what is expected in the workplace will pay great dividends for what comes next. While it may seem like a waste of time to define things that seem obvious, it is not. If you want to have a free flowing creative and innovative workplace you must get this right.

Once definitions are complete, talent and supervisors are to request the executive team to provide definitions of the company values used internally and/or externally that describe the character of the company and talent. These definitions should be in writing preferably, if given at all. Here's where the RUB begins.

If no definitions are provided, the talent and supervisor are to provide their own definitions similar to what was done for the four words and phrase. Core value definitions should be submitted to someone on the executive team for review and comment. Incorporate comments into the final definitions of company core values.

Using the essential language words and term of Trust, Truth, Honesty, Integrity, and Keeping a Confidence objectively assess the upholding of company core values internally and externally at every level of the company's managerial structure (i.e. executive team, V.P.'s, Directors, Managers, Team Leaders, Front Line talent). Where there are significant areas of agreement, celebrate. Where there are significant areas of disagreement, mourn. Where areas are not clear, make note of the sense within the company culture of which side of the cloud would most "prefer."

Reach an agreement at the local level, i.e. within your sphere of influence, to an aspired high standard of company values you and your supervisor are striving toward and hoping to attain. Let those in your sphere know that they should expect, without perfection, you to adhere to the standard. The purpose of adherence is to reflect at the individual talent level character values deemed important to the company that will be objectively and regularly measured, evaluated, and reinforced.

Imagine a workplace where if you said something to a co-worker in confidence you would never expect to see it on a social media account before the end of the day; or ever! Imagine a co-worker of integrity who when hired away by a competitor did not take any of your proprietary information with them to their new job. Imagine someone apologizing in the middle of an important internal sales meeting that they forgot to close the loop with an valued client. Imagine asking for help and being told the truth about what you really needed. Imagine you have a critical deadline to meet and your team says they have your back and you know they "DO." This is what essential language brings into the workplace where truth and knowability are relative to the person.

Creativity and innovation are manifestations of the mind as it puts words and pictures to disperse thoughts and ideas assimilating in the prefrontal cortex of the brain. This occurs most frequently during times of mind leisure where there are no fears, anxious thoughts, or worries occupying the mind. Use of essential language is the driving force for leisure thinking and mindful awareness of surroundings in an authentic and vulnerable workplace.

The way we interact with one another is through verbal and non-verbal means. With essential language established, interactions in communication, cooperation, collaboration, and co-creation can be fluid, fast paced, and supportive toward the common good or objective. The beauty of essential language is that it allows verbal and nonverbal articulation of not just areas of agreement, but conflict areas as well. And while not all conflicts are resolvable, essential language allows each party to know they have been heard.

In some organizations, conflict is intentionally established between two or more groups to help maintain balance between opposing objectives that must be integrated for mutual beneficial success. Without essential language in the workplace and strong company values inherent conflict of opposing objectives would eventually tear the cultural fabric holding the enterprise together. In this Module, the objective is to learn flexibility within a tight standard of care.

Over time, the employee and supervisor replicate the metrics for essential language terms they have agreed upon with each other with others in the workplace. These essential language metrics are embraced, establishing a safe environment of authenticity and vulnerability that allows creativity to flourish and innovation to soar throughout the workplace. How wonderful would it be to work in a place and know at least "here" that up means up, yes means yes, and no means no. A place where, when you are empowering someone to do something, you can trust it's a done deal, and if it can't be done, you'll be the first to know. If you have an issue to be kept in confidence, you don't read it on Twitter before leaving for the day. This listing could be nearly endless. And it is possible to have that environment in the workplace.

Module 3 – Alignment

Alignment of talent personality and temperament with their position and assignments optimizes engagement, productivity, and loyalty at all stages of a work/life career path. Alignment is a continual process of evaluation, feedback, and support as vocational development is validated. Alignment ultimately results in advancement.

In preparation for this Module, talent would complete a company approved or well recognized personality and temperament general assessment that provides a detailed report. This initial assessment exercise provides a baseline profile which can be later updated with job specific assessments including 360 degree profiles. Some of the most recognized general assessments that can expand into great depth of detail include Everything Disc; Myers Briggs; CliftonStrengths; Hogan; and Birkman.

Unleash The Millennials and Save the World

The first read of the assessment report is to make a broad evaluation of the findings in contrast to talent self-perception of what the report is identifying. Assessment reports are generally automated text responses to specific answers and patterns of answers. While they can get in the ballpark, the ability of any assessment to fully illuminate an individual's personality and temperament is debatable. With that in mind the talent is to read the entire report with a pen and colored marker in hand and flag and highlight areas of agreement and disagreement with the findings report. The objective of this review is to recognize and validate areas of agreement and areas where the talent believes they differ with the findings.

Next, the talent identifies areas of alignment and potential misalignment between the personality profile and temperament findings with their own job description and responsibilities. This is the time talent really needs to identify aspirational desires versus rational observations of hard wiring in regard to their current assignment and career path goals. Does the position they hold, the duties they are to fulfill, and the career path they are on match the areas of agreement in the assessment report they affirm.

Often the reality of taking a position is based upon wanting a great job and accepting a position that seems to fit. And at other times, the objective is to just get any job that pays the bills and hopefully survive whatever comes down the chute until a position upgrade can be made. Of course, this is from the talent's perspective.

Typically, the talent does not know if the hiring is done to just fill a slot no matter who walks in the door or if a specific skill set is needed. It is not until a few weeks after settling into a position do both parties involved discover if the talent and position are going to work out. And often a ninety-day grace period to establish compatibility of person with position is articulated by the hiring human resources representative.

The purpose of EPL coaching is to optimize engagement, productivity, and loyalty of talent in the workplace. It is critical for the talent to identify for themselves if they are aligned from a hard wiring personality and temperament perspective with their position and career path or do they now view themselves as a square peg trying to fit into a round hole. Either observation is positive. If alignment is validated, talent can begin the process of fully embracing their position and career path. If significant misalignment is identified, talent can begin to identify adjustments to find a position and career path more properly aligned with their hard wiring.

Following the talent report review and findings self-evaluation they should meet with their direct supervisor and discuss their assessment. The point of this meeting is to either identify where position and duties can be tweaked to address areas of minor misalignment or to identify other potential positions within the organization that can be migrated toward over time for major misalignment.

Rarely does this exercise indicate a perfect match and that is to be expected. At the end of the supervisor session, the talent and supervisor identify workarounds where minor misalignments are noted, and what to do in cases of misalignments that are not easily overcome. The end goal is to get talent in a position along a career path where they can comfortably play, master, and discover aligned with their hard wiring.

Module 4 – Engagement

The Engagement Module focuses on how to attain vocational competency and cultivate creativity in the workplace. Linkage between engagement building competency that cultivates creativity is related to emotional commitment and empowerment. We will explore at the end of this section why engagement is a major contributor to the discovery of life meaning in the workplace.

In this module, the coach helps talent articulate their engagement experience as determined by metrics and measurements (M&M) for engagement in his/her position. Positional duty specific M&M's can be developed and used in place of the very broad emotionally based M&M's used herein.

During the post M&M assessment evaluation, coach and talent review engagement drivers to determine which are in place within the workplace and if they are meaningful or beneficial to talent duties. For those areas where the talent engagement is lacking a full list of engagement drivers should be reviewed to see if the any drivers not currently in place could increase meaningful engagement.

For Module 4, we will only use M&M's for what would be identified as the top positional duty. The decision to limit our selection to one is the short time-window of the Module. In a long-term scenario, all top areas

Unleash The Millennials and Save the World

of positional duties would be addressed to ensure optimal alignment. Use of only "the" top positional duty reflects an application of a common 80/20 rule. It would not be unexpected that eighty percent of engagement effort is spent in twenty percent of Positional Duties.

Engagement is a function of consistent alignment AND experience of emotional commitment and empowerment applied in positional duties in the workplace. It does not occur in a vacuum but within a supportive workplace framework where open and transparent communication of measured metric results are assessed, evaluated, and feedback provided. Metric measurement, assessment, and feedback are inseparably linked to engagement enhancement, development, productivity, and advancement.

We will consider three levels of Engagement in Module 4; engaged, not-engaged, and actively disengaged. Engaged would reflect consistency in high levels of emotional commitment and empowerment metrics and appropriate time dedicated to Positional Duties. Not Engaged would reflect inconsistency in levels of emotional commitment and empowerment metrics and inconsistency in time dedicated to Positional Duties. And finally, Actively Disengaged would reflect a low level of emotional commitment and empowerment metrics and lack of time dedicated to Positional Duties.

When talent looks back on self-completed assignments for Modules 1 to 3, they will soon recognize that it is unlikely they will be engaged and empowered in all duties and assigned tasks of their current position. The Baseline Coaching sheet and resultant Game Board (Module 1) should be a first broad-brush indicator of what talent can expect for power areas of engagement. Module 2, essential language and company core values will illuminate "value" areas of conflict that impact engagement. Module 3, personality and temperament alignment with position and duties illuminates' areas we all share; being hard wired to seamlessly mesh with some things and diametrically opposed to others.

Metrics for the role of emotional commitment in engagement are self-measurements of time and emotionally based criteria. Metrics for the role of empowerment in engagement are self-evaluations of "comfort level" in terms of responsibility and authority for the positional duty being assessed. All metrics with the exception of time are subjectively determined by the talent.

Subjectivity is viewed in the example herein as a positive given the point of the exercise is to provide talent with the best measure of their own EPL; i.e. their own "feelings and inklings." While we can power through and put up with most things optimal performance and work/life balance is achieved when work is a natural and pleasing outflow from within a person and not something forced or ill-fitting.

Objective assessment of contact time with positional duties does not mean there was engagement specifically, but that time was spent where engagement could have occurred. Actual engagement would be reflected in the emotional commitment and empowerment exercised during positional duty contact time.

Empowerment is typically a function of delegated responsibility and authority. For Module 4, the observations of empowerment observations should be discussed, and clarity of positional empowerment established with talent direct supervisor.

For validation of self-assessment findings, it is strongly suggested to have a direct supervisor independently observe and monitor talent "engagement" for a given block of time within the window of time talent is self-evaluating. Following observation and compilation of talent measurement and assessment, the self-assessment findings should be presented to the talent supervisor for review.

The end result is to have relative certainty of the level of engagement in the top positional duty. Where engagement is occurring, talent is to continue to regularly assess and align for sustainability. If it is found for positional duty that talent was not engaged, it is important to determine underlying causes effecting emotional commitment and empowerment. It may be something very simple and an area for future development.

Any finding of active disengagement is an immediate red flag not just for engagement, but also for productivity in position and loyalty to company and vocation. The importance of Module 2 in helping to bring transparency and communication to areas of active disengagement cannot be overemphasized. This is not something to hide, but rather to expose and allow to be effectively resolved. While active disengagement can be ignored or swept under the rug on the least important positional duties without much immediate consequence, on one of the top duties it needs to be resolved quickly.

Unleash The Millennials and Save the World

At the end of each day, using the top positional duty as the area of engagement focus, talent is to record M&M's (see listing below). First is the approximate time spent on the top duty. Next, using a one to ten scale of low to high, talent is to rate their "sense" of experiencing two emotional based labor metrics (use same two metrics throughout evaluation). Finally, using the one to ten scale, talent is to rate their "sense" of experiencing happiness while performing the top positional duty. If they do not spend any time on the top duty on any given day they respond with an N/A in the appropriate fields. This is a daily recording for two consecutive weeks for Module 4. An example completed worksheet follows the metrics list.

Engagement Metrics for Emotional Commitment
Time
Emotional Based (pick two to measure for evaluation duration)
    Satisfaction-in completing
    Enjoyment of doing
    Experiencing "good" as a reward
    Enjoyment of financial gain/pay
    "Time flying by" with "joy in your heart"
Happiness

EXAMPLE COMPLETED EMOTIONAL COMMITMENT WORKSHEET												
Time and Metric Observations for Performing THE Positional Duty	Week 1					Week 2						
	D1	D2	D3	D4	D5	D1	D2	D3	D4	D5	Total	Avg
Time (Hours)	5	3	4	4	7	2	2	6	4	5	42	4.2
Rate your "Experience" performing Duty on a 0 to 10 scale (10 highest)												
Emotional Based (Rate 2 Daily)	D1	D2	D3	D4	D5	D1	D2	D3	D4	D5	Total	Avg
Satisfaction in Completing	--	--	--	--	--	--	--	--	--	--	na	na
Enjoyment of Doing	9	8	6	6	9	6	7	10	8	6	75	7.5
Experiencing "Good" for Doing	--	--	--	--	--	--	--	--	--	--	na	na
Enjoyment of Financial Gain/Pay	--	--	--	--	--	--	--	--	--	--	na	na
"Time flying by" with "joy in your heart"	10	9	5	6	10	6	7	10	9	6	78	7.8
Happiness (Rate Daily)	D1	D2	D3	D4	D5	D1	D2	D3	D4	D5		
Internal Happiness	10	9	5	6	10	6	7	10	9	5	77	7.7
Total	29	26	16	18	29	18	21	30	26	17		
Average	9.7	8.7	5.3	6.0	9.7	6.0	7.0	10.0	8.7	5.7		

For the example engagement worksheet shown above the following are evaluation criteria. In regard to time, four hours or more in performing the top positional duty indicates sufficient time was available for

EPL Coaching | Gateway to Creativity and Innovation

"engagement" to occur. Times of less than fours and greater than two hours may hinder engagement in top positional due to influence of other obligations. Two hours or less on top positional duty makes it very difficult to engage in activities due to other responsibilities.

For the emotional commitment metrics for subjective ratings of "feelings and inklings" evaluate using the average of row totals to the far right of the table. Averages greater than eight are considered engaged; less than eight and more than four are considered not-engaged; and less than four hours are considered actively disengaged.

The average time for emotional commitment measurement of the talent in the example above to be reflective of actual engagement occurring is on the low side of assurance (4.2 hours). Seven of the ten days measured, the talent spent four or more hours on the top positional duty. The three remaining days, while time was spent, the opportunity to be engaged in the top duty is questionable.

Using the emotional commitment metric averages (i.e. 7.5, 7.8, 7.7), the talent would be considered "not engaged" in the top positional duty. Questions to answer for this example would include: What was difference between engaged days and not engaged days? What positional duty adjustments would improve emotional commitment column totals average? and, What development would improve emotional commitment?

Next we will briefly look at the empowerment metrics. For the top positional duty being evaluated talent first must establish their own understanding of the scope and boundaries of their responsibility and the related authority for fulfilling their duty. Both can be unlimited or restricted depending upon the circumstances. Owners and top executives would likely have relatively unlimited scopes and boundaries while these diminish with each layer down the chain of command.

This calls for a discussion with the supervisor to clearly delineate and define if possible, scope and boundaries for both responsibility and authority. Once delineated and defined, metric measurement can begin.

Using the top positional duty as the area of empowerment focus, at the end of each day talent is to record the approximate time spent on each Task. Time is simply used to tie the two engagement worksheets together (i.e. measuring metrics of two sheets for same engagement periods). They then record their "sense" on a 1 to 10 scale of their subjective "feelings and inklings" regarding confidence levels for exercising their delineated and defined responsibility and authority. These metrics for confidence levels are shown below. An example completed worksheet follows.

Engagement Metrics for Empowerment
Responsibility and Authority (R&A) use Same Confidence Metrics
   Clear/Transparent   (i.e. No questions)
   Cloudy (i.e. Not sure but was able to exercise R&A))
   Turbid (i.e. No clue and stopped work)

EXAMPLE COMPLETED EMPOWERMENT WORKSHEET												
Observations of Clarity of R&E Performing The Positional Duty	Week 1					Week 2						
	D1	D2	D3	D4	D5	D1	D2	D3	D4	D5	Total	Avg
Time (hours)	5	3	4	4	7	2	2	6	4	5	42	4.2
Rate "Experience" of all three criteria (0 to 10) while performing Duty (Totals: R = 10; A=10; R+A=20)												
Responsibility	D1	D2	D3	D4	D5	D1	D2	D3	D4	D5	Total	Avg
Clear/Transparent (i.e. No questions)	9	9	7	7	9	6	7	10	9	8	81	8.1
Cloudy (i.e. Not sure but was able to work)	1	1	3	2	1	4	3	0	1	1	17	1.7
Turbid (i.e. No clue and stopped work)	0	0	0	1	0	0	0	0	0	1	2	0.2
Authority	D1	D2	D3	D4	D5	D1	D2	D3	D4	D5		
Clear/Transparent (i.e. No questions)	10	8	6	7	10	8	8	10	10	8	85	8.5
Cloudy (i.e. Not sure but was able to work)	0	2	4	2	0	2	2	0	0	2	14	1.4
Turbid (i.e. No clue and stopped work)	0	0	0	1	0	0	0	0	0	0	1	0.1

For the example Empowerment worksheet the metric that counts is the row total averages to the far right of the table for Clear/Transparent metric for both Responsibility and Authority. For this metric an average total of more than eight is considered engaged; less than eight and greater than four is not engaged; and less than four is actively disengaged

This example indicates talent is experiencing Empowerment engagement (i.e. 8.1 and 8.5) in their top Positional Duty measured. Questions to answer for both Responsibility and Authority would include: "On those days when Clarity was not present what were apparent causes?" "What adjustments in Positional Duty(s) would improve Clarity?" And, What development would improve Empowerment Clarity?

When talent is experiencing Engagement in terms of both emotional commitment and empowerment the rate of talent going from vocational competence to proficiency is greatly accelerated. Talent loves what they do and increasingly becomes more proficient accomplishing their duties.

Over-time, as optimal proficiency is approached it fosters talent to begin to explore creative ways to accomplish their duties. They take what

EPL Coaching | Gateway to Creativity and Innovation

had become a bland and fading fabric of their duties and add flavor, color, and new patterns accomplishing increasingly more consistent and tightly fitted outcomes in duties of mounting complexity.

When a person is experiencing Engagement in their work life takes on real and heart felt meaning. There is rich internal feedback and positive feelings when they know not only what to do but enjoy creative expression in doing. Work becomes not just something they do for others, although positive feedback from others is likely increasing, but is something they do for themselves. There is a reason someone coined the colloquialism, "If you love what you do, you will never work a day in your life." They were letting the rest of us know what they discovered about those who experience life meaning in their work.

Module 5 – Productivity

The Productivity Module focuses on attaining vocational mastery and fostering innovation in the workplace. Linkage between mastery and innovation, as with engagement and creativity, is related to emotional commitment and empowerment. We will also explore at the end of this section why vocational productivity is a major contributor to the discovery of life purpose in the workplace.

Similar to the Engagement Module, the top positional productivity element is used as the basis for evaluating productivity over a two-week interval. Productivity metrics and measurements will be used to prepare a findings report presented to and discussed with a Supervisor.

Productivity is a function and/or a consequence of actuating results and outcomes of intentional or unintentional actions. It can be both linear and non-linear and have positive and negative effects. For purposes of this Module, we will define productivity as results of actions taken by aligned emotionally committed and empowered talent or teams of talent within in a supportive workplace framework environment. While productivity is often considered time dependent, time can be a minor component when considering results of actions in the Connected Age of data and technology.

We will consider three levels of productivity in Module 5, productive; not-productive; and actively un-productive. Productive would reflect consistency in high levels of emotional commitment and empowerment metrics while producing desired results at or above expectations. Not-productive would reflect inconsistency in levels of emotional commitment and empowerment metrics while producing desired results at or below expectations. And finally, actively un-productive would reflect a low level of emotional commitment and empowerment metrics while producing undesirable results.

The metrics for measuring emotional commitment in productivity are the same self-measurements as in the engagement module of emotionally based criteria and actual time dedicated to actuation of desired results from actions taken. Metrics for empowerment part of productivity are self-evaluations of three "confidence levels" in terms of responsibility and authority for actions taken to create desired results. These confidence levels include comfortable (having full ease and confidence of taking actions); uncomfortable (not having full ease and confidence of taking actions); and immobile (no ease and no confidence of taking actions).

There are no example worksheets for productivity as the metrics and measurement criteria are the same as the engagement module with the exception of the new empowerment metrics for productivity mentioned in the prior paragraph. Evaluations of the recorded results would use the same numeric standards found in the engagement module.

Objective assessment of contact time with positional duties does not mean there was productivity specifically, but that time was spent where productivity could have occurred. Actual productivity would be reflected in the emotional commitment and empowerment exercised during positional duty contact time where desired results occur from actions taken.

For validation of self-assessment findings, a direct supervisor should independently observe and monitor talent "productivity" for a given block of time within the window of time talent is self-evaluating. Following observation and compilation of measurement and assessment findings the supervisor should be presented a findings report for review and discussion.

The end result is for talent to have relative certainty of their level of productivity in their top positional duty. Where productivity is occurring continue to regularly assess and align for sustainability. If it is discovered talent is not-productive in their positional duty it is important to determine underlying causes effecting emotional commitment and

EPL Coaching | Gateway to Creativity and Innovation

empowerment. It may be something very simple and an area for future development. It may also indicate a larger underlying issue in other areas not assessed.

Any finding of actively un-productive is an immediate red flag not just for productivity, but also for engagement in position and loyalty to company and vocation. The importance of Module 2 in helping to bring transparency and communication to areas of actively un-productive cannot be overemphasized. This is not something to hide, but rather to expose and allow to be effectively resolved. While actively un-productive can be ignored or swept under the rug on the least important positional duties without much immediate consequence, on one of th top duties it needs to be resolved quickly.

When talent experiences productivity in terms of both emotional commitment and empowerment the rate of talent reaching vocational mastery is greatly quickened. Talent loves taking actions that create desired results all the while overcoming known and unforeseen challenges. They work on developing new skills while honing old ones to increase the effectiveness of actions taken to create better results than expected. The pinnacle of mastery formulation is when talent can seamless train others toward mastery.

Over-time, as optimal mastery is approached, talent begins to push the envelope of possibility and begin to innovate completely new ways to create above and beyond results. They not only know what and how to do what is currently required but also the underlying productivity motivations for what they do. Stepping back and looking solely at the motivations they are able to envision new connections of mechanics and technology for assimilation, integration, and synthesis of entirely new innovations to satisfy motivations. They will transform long held paradigms into a memory as they innovate disruptor means of productivity. In a word—revolutionary.

When a person is experiencing Productivity in their work purpose in life manifests. Purpose is what drives us all to go the edge without fear of what we will discover there. Purpose supersedes in many instances the value of one's own life in comparison to the fulfillment of that purpose. Purpose is why fireman run into burning buildings, law enforcement runs toward the gun fire, and a mother or father jump in front of an approaching vehicle to push their child out of harm's way. If you ever wonder why some people die quickly after retirement and others never retire and keep living going to work you'll discover knowing one's purpose, as well as life meaning, are huge influence factors.

Module 6 – Loyalty

Loyalty Module focuses on sustaining workplace and vocational loyalty for the purpose of establishing talent as recognized and respected vocational authorities. Connection between sustaining loyalty and manifesting authority is directly related to engagement and productivity and their respective empowerment and emotional commitment metrics and measurements. Workplace and vocational loyalty are major contributors to the discovery of life calling.

The coaching session for Module 6 is relatively straight forward and related to awareness of sustaining time in workplace and vocation, obtaining extensive knowledge of workplace and vocational fundamental institutional knowledge, and exercising discernment and wisdom concerning interrelationships of the myriad influencing workplaces and vocations.

The purpose of this Module is not to prepare individuals to be the top executives in their company, although this may be a by-product, but rather to motivate them to become chief Authorities in their vocation locally, regionally, and nationally. Vocations are advanced by visionary Authorities taking center stage and while exercising great humility inspiring others to become motivated and engage to be vocationally productive.

It is a pretty simple exercise. Coaches challenge talent to identify their time spent in current workplace and vocation and their confidence in an extended career path that may last a life-time. Next is identification of workplace and vocational institutional knowledge known and what is lacking that can be gained in the next three years. And finally, identification of currently held professional organization memberships and those memberships that would add to their sphere of acquiring knowledge and making connections.

Putting into motion the obtaining of what talent is missing and desirous of pursuing is the Module assignment. Talent should meet with their supervisor to seek assistance and guidance to navigate internally on their quest. For vocational assistance and guidance, talent should approach local and regional recognized and respected authorities to make a connection and begin a vocationally rewarding relationship.

While there are many opportunities to do many different things vocationally, individually we are best suited for relatively few. And discovery of one of those few and continuing in it provides evidence of a life calling. Life calling is not to be good at many things but master of none. We were created to engage with purpose and discover thru experience where our life calling will lead us.

Personally, my life calling has involved many different workplaces and educational stops along the way but has always centered around helping people achieve above and beyond what they thought possible. Most recently this has been through my executive coaching practice. Even now, I sense the writing of this book is opening a new and more expansive door to exercise my calling.

Module 7 – Sustainability

The purpose of Module 7 is for the talent to review with the coach a summary of all the metrics and measurements and explain how the process evolved over time. The coach then asks the talent to suggest ideas for how to sustain the process moving forward, with the support of the supervisor. Also, the coach and talent discuss ways to have conversations with others in the workplace about ways to explain the M&M process to them. Finally, the talent completes a new Baseline Survey that will be used to measure the effectiveness of the coaching program and allow the coach to tweak program deficiencies for the future.

End of Module Summaries.

As noted at the beginning of this Chapter this is not a one size fits all program. The Module summaries are meant as guides to possibilities for enhancing EPL in the workplace. In particular, Essential Language Module 2 is so critical to everything in the workplace that I want to go into that one in more detail. The Module 2 essential language terms (trust, truth, honesty, integrity, and keeping a confidence) are interconnected and vital if talent are to securely learn "knowable things." They are also vital in order to foster the authenticity and vulnerability that, in turn, fosters creativity and innovation.

As an example, suppose someone defines workplace "trust" to mean that someone can "see" and "feel" that known expectations of behavior and communications are being maintained (i.e. "metrics"). Now when something happens in the workplace that requires trust, both parties have a mutual understanding of what trust requires. And when trust is either maintained or broken according to the definition, they have clarity of communication when they address the situation. Of course, this definition will be completely subjective between the parties, as will all definitions, based upon whatever standard of reference is selected. Without transcendent foundations, ideas and concepts are not stable and should not be assumed so. However, the more individuals who can agree on a single definition, the more support it will have without losing any of its subjectivity.

We are currently living in a world of Postmodern skepticism that promotes the idea that nothing is true, and nothing is knowable. Now this sounds great and is good for those desiring to use whatever means are necessary to get what they want. While there have been, are, will always be leaks, liars, cheats, thugs, those who envy, and diabolical people in every large group of people, you certainly don't want them populating your workplace and having their way. This is not a Millennial issue only, as we all fail miserably in each of the essential language areas unless we hold ourselves accountable to others to uphold trust, truth, honesty, integrity, and keeping a confidence in accordance with agreed upon metrics. At least if we all agree that the metric for trust is only applicable sixty percent of the time we know where we stand when I'm told by my supervisor to trust my position is secure. Does this sound as ridiculous and sad and true to read as it was to write? Without a transcendent foundation this is our reality.

This EPL Coaching program is specifically designed for enhancing talent creativity and innovation in the workplace and providing meaning, purpose, and affirmation of the talent' vocational calling. I encourage you to discover coaching, bring it into your organization, and allow it to add beautiful colors to your cultural and talent fabric.

EPL Coaching | Gateway to Creativity and Innovation

What are you to do with Millennials once they are optimally aligned in EPL and are being creatively innovative in the workplace? I am so glad you asked. That is what I've been developing for my clients in my coaching practice. Unleash The Millennials and Save the World.

Unleash The Millennials and Save the World

Chapter 19

Unleashing the Millennials | Begin to Save the World

In light of the acceleration of the millennium change cycle (MCC), when the resultant MCC tsunami crests around 2025 the completion of the paradigm transformation from Industrial Age to Connected Age business models will occur seemingly overnight. Those businesses that are not ready for the change will not survive. In these final chapters, I will show you how to get started. I sincerely want you to succeed and am providing you the game plan for success in this chapter.

The game plan elements are presented in a bullet list below, which will be expanded on briefly in the rest of the chapter. I've introduced them in the order I'd recommend, but there is no secret to the order. Do first what is your highest priority in your organization; but do them all.

> **Innovation Catalyst Coaching:** Introduction of coaching throughout the organization and engagement, productivity, and loyalty (EPL) coaching for all key Millennial talent; individual and/or in group sessions.
>
> **Next Generation Leader (NGL) Initiative:** Intentionally train, in the business of your business, Xer and Millennial talent who will step up as leaders in your organization in three to five years (e.g. team, group, department, division).

Unleash The Millennials and Save the World

Millennial Dream Team Formation: For each business unit, assemble an innovation team led by a top Millennial surrounded by key holders of institutional knowledge in your company. Their goal is to innovate their area of your existing business such that, when finished, your future business will be one with which your current business could not dream of competing!

Leadership Optimization: Do an objective, top to bottom evaluation of current leadership and optimize those positions with Connected Age savvy and gritty talent.

Institutional Knowledge (IK) Transfer: Initiate IK transfer coaching between holders of key IK and succession candidates, to capture what is in the mind and heart and identify what is in the files and servers… and what isn't but needs to be.

Succession Implementation: Time for the Boomers over 62 to recognize the time has arrived to begin preparing their successors and starting the process.

Innovation Catalyst Coaching: The primary drivers for Millennial EPL are vocational development, advancement opportunities, and work/life balance. With that in mind, the foremost priority within the Connected Age business model paradigm is the introduction of coaching throughout the organization to develop Millennial talent and help them advance in an environment of authenticity and truth that drives creativity and innovation while experiencing work/life balance. This is not another layer of administrative oversight but a best practices method that achieves proven results. It also replaces an Industrial Age employee review process.

The most general level of coaching for all talent is what I call baseline coaching. This type of coaching immediately follows on-boarding training for new talent and annual reviews (or quarterly or whatever you do) for current talent. Baseline coaching includes having talent identify and articulate their position purpose, objectives of position, recurring activities, challenges, the results their position creates, and desired outcome of results achievement for the employee. Initially, the employee articulates to the coach his/her understanding of individual responsibilities in each of these areas. The employee then confirms his/her ideas about his/her duties with the appropriate supervisors and peers and reports back to the coach. With verified information, the coach then has the employee develop a plan to achieve the desired results, to be submitted to the managing supervisor for review, feedback, and approval. Once approved (it may take some edits), the employee provides updates about progress to the supervisor at regular intervals. Supervisor feedback is addressed during the next coaching session to modify the plan if needed.

Benchmark coaching is talent initial foray into owning their development and advancement in the realm of creativity and innovation as they map out their own path forward. With regular check-ins with their coaches and supervisors to ensure they are flying at the proper altitude and direction; they are able to correct and/or adjust any deficiencies along the way.

What does a review look like after baseline coaching is complete? The employee reports to his/her supervisor this way: This is what I said I would do. Here are the challenges that popped up. These are my ideas to overcome challenges. Here are my results. These are tasks where I found strength and alignment. These are areas I can improve. These are areas of weakness I need to protect against. These are technical tools I found that work. These are technical tools I need to improve my position. This is how I am aligned in regard to my career path. This is my plan for the next review cycle. The supervisor's role is to assess and evaluate the employee's ability and the adjustments made in the process. This helps the supervisor help the employee realize his/her goals.

The next level of coaching also works at all levels and is the EPL Coaching I mentioned in the previous chapter. EPL Coaching is aimed at supercharging your top talent to create and innovate, teaching them how to coach their peers and show them how to replicate the enhanced EPL for creativity and innovation. Top talent is difficult to find, and, once hired, important to preserve, develop, and Unleash. EPL Coaching infuses the values of life meaning, individual purpose, and vocational calling into the critical principles of workplace engagement, productivity, and loyalty. This coaching program develops incredibly strong bonds between the coached talent and their peers, and also with their supervisors. It most effectively aligns and promotes vocational and professional development and career path advancement.

Finally, executive coaching, as mentioned earlier, has been a best practice method for emotional integration and leadership development for almost twenty years in large global corporations. We all have emotional states, whether as part of our personality or as a result of life experience. We carry those emotions with us into critical business encounters. It is imperative that talent at the executive level are aware of and strive to maintain healthy emotional integration in all areas of their life—all of which coaching addresses. In the area of leadership development, coaches work with executives to help them articulate their outcomes, purpose, values, and vision and develop strategic plans to ensure their own creativity and innovation is fully energized and effective in achieving positive results.

Next Generation Leader (NGL) Initiative: What exactly does your organization do to train future project/program managers and leaders in your organization "before" and "after" they assume a leadership position? Are current project/program managers/leaders in your organization fully aware of their position's parameters? Do they know the clear limits of responsibility and authority? And finally, are communications, continuity, and metrics and measurements in place to ensure adherence to corporate standards in all areas for project/program managers/leaders in your organization?

In view of these questions and the problematic fact that Xer middle management is missing, the impending crest of the MCC tsunami, and the continuing roll-out from the workplace of retiring Boomers, developing and launching an NGL Initiative within your company for select Millennials and Xers is a must. The purpose of the NGL Initiative is to develop masterful Millennial and Xer talent to be your next generation leaders. This ensures leadership succession and company growth. Developing these leaders is accomplished by effectively, but humbly, communicating with and educating the next leaders about the skills, knowledge, and expertise necessary for them to gain mastery in the business of your business, their technical vocation, people soft skills, and HR compliance. Mastery in one or more of these areas will enhance movement along career paths within the company. It will also help with the institutional knowledge transfer for leadership succession. The NGL Initiative uses internal mentors/coaches to model your unique company culture and inspire others to do the same. At the senior leadership level, communication, cooperation, collaboration, co-creation (C4), and participation are critical skills to model consistently for the next generation of leaders.

The NGL Initiative follows a simple cycle of guidance, reassurance, and confidence. Guidance relates to telling your NGLs why you do something and showing them how your organization does it (i.e. training modules and group mentoring). Reassurance is the process of group coaching NGLs to get them started doing the same and keep them going and growing. Confidence is the process of group coaching NGLs to help them reproduce in others what they have learned. Learning becomes mastery when we can teach others. Talent have mastered their vocation when they can train others to become masterful.

The NGL Initiative must be a top down program benefiting all participants in the initiative whether they are a front-line department manager or a Millennial talent with only a couple years' experience. The NGL Initiative is intended to infuse Module contents and an expressed desire for creativity and innovation throughout the entire workplace culture. It becomes woven into the fabric of everyday life, not a one-and-done and forgotten training waste of time. The short-term objective is for the engaging training sessions and follow-up mentor/coach and NGL team meetings to disrupt work as minimally as possible (e.g. lunch and learns). The positive impacts of the initiative on talent and the business will ensure the sustainability of the program. The NGL Initiative is conducted with complete transparency. Individual performance and recommendations from supervisors dictate who is invited to participate.

Once the participants are identified and invited to join the NGL Initiative and mentor/coach and NGL teams are assigned, the training can begin. Each month a new training module of the company's choosing is presented for the purpose of providing three primary takeaways for the NGLs: What was taught? Why is it important? and How is it applied in what I do?

The mentor/coach and NGL teams meet on another day to discuss the module. Initially, the mentor/coach leads the discussion to obtain NGL feedback. Once feedback is received, the mentor/coach demonstrates how what was taught applies to their own position by providing real examples of their own work to the NGLs. Then, using the coaching process, the mentor/coach helps the NGLs discover, in their own positions, the implications of the presentation. All feedback is collected, assimilated, and synthesized in a summary report to the participants of the NGL Initiative.

Millennial Dream Team Formation: This is a top tier exercise for maximum creation and innovation of your business or business line by the formation of a Millennial Dream Team (MDT). It begins with the identification of your top performing Millennial(s) on your staff and surrounding them with at least one senior executive of your choosing and senior level leaders of their choosing from each of your core business of the business areas (i.e. technical, finance, operations, and sales/marketing). The team is headed by the Millennial. The senior executive's role, beyond participation, is veto power over any team decisions for innovation moving forward. In the event of a veto, the CEO and/or executive team are asked to evaluate the innovation and rule on the veto being lifted or remaining in place.

The purpose of the MDT is three-fold. First, to look closely at all areas of your business and create and innovate optimization plans to fully transform each into the Connected Age business model paradigm. In other words, the team will identify deficiencies and provide innovative pathways to reach standards that will allow the business to thrive tomorrow and into the future, past the MCC tsunami. Second, to look closely at the business and create an innovation that so vastly improves your business performance in terms of market share, total revenue, and net income that your competitors will have to make rapid and similar innovations in order to remain viable. It is not a matter of if, but when this will happen in your business sector. Third, to have the MDT look closely at the motivations behind your business sector and create and innovate a disruptor business that satisfies the motivations in an entirely new Connected Age way, i.e. eliminating the need for your current business altogether. Here is the reality, someone is already likely working on this type of disruptor in your business sector and the MDT could identify what that disruptor may look like, providing forewarning and an opportunity to become that disruptor and thus stay in business.

Unleashing the Millennials | Begin to Save the World

The MDT's goal is the elimination of outdated technologies and software with a shift to specific AI tools, computing, and storage available from the myriad of cloud computing vendors. Establishment of new best practices procedures includes virtual learning for every area of the business, from on-boarding to technical training and development. All of this is to ensure you don't end up in a disruptor market and become another Blockbusters, Kodak, or Borders Books. Amazon started their disrupter in 1994. What can you start today?

It is simple and sweet. Millennials see and perceive things differently because they do not have forty or fifty years of out-of-date baggage to carry regarding what can and cannot be done. Having a Millennial in charge of a creative team within your organization, supported by your top talent, and focused on innovation, is the best strategy to really see something significant happen. They are at the cusp. They are the first generation to actively be involved in implementing AI technologies in every sector of life. Gen-Z following them will grow up with AI and take it well beyond our imagination today. Your top Millennial will be doing this five-years from now so why not Unleash The Millennials early and let them get started to save your business today, and, while they're at it, begin to Save the World.

<u>Leadership Optimization:</u> This is a very sensitive subject but one that needs to be addressed if you want to create and innovate. Leadership optimization will ensure creativity and innovation is being thought about and planned at all levels of leadership within an organization. The outcome of leadership optimization is an expectation within the organization from every top-level position of leadership that creativity and innovation are important aspects of the normal course of business. Once this expectation reaches the masses, there will be an upswelling of energy and anticipation.

Given the sensitivity of this process it is important to introduce the concept to your leadership team(s) in realistic terms. This is not a succession plan to push anyone out or replace them. It is, rather, an offer of more resources to empower these leaders to do even more. Most leaders know when technological and market advances exceed their know-how and comfort level. If you can assure them that the next generation leader pool is here now to both help and learn, current leadership will feel empowered, not threatened. The creative innovation process is to produce positive results for the organization, and current leadership will direct and manage the roll-out of that innovation if approved.

Starting at the top of the organization (i.e. CEO/President and immediate reports), the executive team should articulate and map out a strategic plan that includes creativity and innovation within their empowerment areas. This plan should next be reviewed and improved upon by the next level of key leaders in the organization. And finally, front line supervisors are provided with the most recently updated creativity and innovation strategic plan. Their job is to address the practicality and workplace impact of the strategic plan and suggest areas for further study if warranted.

Over a period of six months or less, depending upon the size of the organization, a top down and bottom up creativity and innovation strategic plan initiated by the executive team is available for them to act upon. Then simply pull the trigger. The fun in any workplace is not the difficulty of the task at hand but jointly sharing in the positive results.

Institutional Knowledge (IK) Transfer: Think about your organization. Are all your operational documents current, in digital form, and in accordance with the most up-to-date best practices? Who are the walking repositories of critical company history, work experience, and client contacts that have not yet been written down? If an employee with critical IK were no longer around, what irreplaceable IK would be lost that would make it difficult for the company to move forward?

With these questions in mind, and the leadership optimization exercise just covered, the formation of a Millennial Dream Team is a high priority. Provide talent with key IK the opportunity to pick their top Millennial talent and empower them to lead the creativity and innovation effort in their area. Those IK-holding employees need to be charged with revealing to their Millennial team leader their wealth of institutional knowledge before they walk out of the door with that knowledge untapped. Recognize that your company has invested in people who have accumulated and stored that IK in their brains. It was not so that it would pay back zero in return for their waiting for retirement. Let a Millennial do something with it and the Boomer enjoy seeing their accumulated IK result in creative innovation.

Unleashing the Millennials | Begin to Save the World

Another marker of the coming MCC tsunami crest is the widespread disappearance of key IK. After the tsunami crest many organizations will basically be starting where they are and keep moving forward without the benefit of knowing what used to be known. Paper will be a thing that is recycled, technology will all be cloud based, and what is known by your talent is all that is known apart from the cloud. So, start the process of accessing it now.

Succession Implementation: Succession is a scary topic to bring up in a room full of Boomer executives. "We're being replaced," they will think. I've learned to introduce the topic in terms of the reality of the workplace which likely makes their replacement doubtful until retirement. As a position is vacated above, someone below is either moved up or an external candidate is selected to fill the position. The filling of this one vacant spot at the top internally may have at least two or more chairs below needing to be filled. The lack of internal training and dearth of Xers in middle management makes finding lower level replacements difficult. When they hear that, eyes open around the room. Soon the room buzzes about the need to develop talent to ensure that smooth succession happens at all levels. Their next step is typically instituting an NGL Initiative in their organization.

What frightened Boomers still working have collectively failed to recognize is that there are not enough qualified candidates to fill all the positions about to be vacated by Boomers. It is not like there are rooms full of Xers in organizations itching to sit in the chairs at the next level. There are a few, but Xers the Boomers are fearing will take their chairs were never born. This problem will be painfully evident soon enough.

So, what is a chair sitter and a company supposed to do? Identify top Millennial talent first. Assign a Millennial who is envisioned for a particular position an EPL coach specifically to prepare him/her. The goal is to be made professionally ready for the specific career opportunity while being aligned with their vision and passion. Allow the Millennial to participate in your organization's NGL Initiative to learn the business of your business. Then relax and allow that Millennial to start learning about your IK vault of treasures. Work with him/her to create and innovate what you know into great products, services, and expanded markets. Have fun!

Unleash The Millennials and Save the World

The next chapter is devoted to rescuing transcendent truth and knowability within the workplace. Culturally, truth and knowability will continue to swirl for a least another decade or so as another philosophic age with theological underpinnings is established. We must together in our collective workspaces recapture transcendent truth and knowability or we may literally not survive what is coming next. Unleash The Millennials and Save the World.

Chapter 20

Truth and Knowability | Value of Company Values

Establishment of truth and knowability in the workplace is critical. For a business to operate properly and profitably, talent at all levels must have a common understanding of objective truth (e.g. A does not equal Non-A) and knowability (e.g. harmful behavior in the workplace is not acceptable). In Chapter 18 on the engagement, productivity, and loyalty (EPL) Coaching program, I noted that establishing a common understanding (e.g. truth and knowability) between talent and their supervisors regarding the essential language metrics of trust, truth, honesty, integrity, and keeping a confidence was an important piece. This is necessary given that we have lost a common understanding of these metrics. Let me give you an example and then I will expand this idea.

Justin is a new hire in an industrial facility. His career path will lead to his becoming a unit operator. His first assignment is to assist a process unit inspection team. The first training Justin receives is how to tag out a breaker box once a process unit is de-energized and before his team enters to conduct the inspection. He is told specifically that the reason for tagging the box is to prevent someone who is unaware of what is happening from passing by, seeing that the breaker is off, resetting the breaker, and frying the workers inside. It is assumed that Justin understands this as a health and safety "truth" and has the cognitive ability to "know" that this is the standard procedure. The process unit must be de-energized at the breaker box and the box tagged out before anyone enters.

The next day, Justin assembles with the crew at another process unit, but Greg, his trainer, who normally tags the breaker box, is out sick. Justin tells the team he knows what to do and they can get their gear ready as he takes care of de-energizing the unit. It took him longer than he thought to find the breaker box and pull the switch but eventually he was successful and de-energized the unit. He then realizes he doesn't have any tags as Greg is the only one on the team authorized to carry tags and tag out breakers. "It was fine yesterday," Justin thinks, "we won't be in there too long; why waste more time getting a tag." He returns to the team smiling and says, "All done, we can go in now."

After they are all in, Joe, also a recent hire, on his way to check in with the shift foreman, sees the open breaker box and that the breaker to the process unit is off. Not thinking too clearly after a late night out, Joe does what he thinks he is supposed to do when he sees a breaker off in his area that is not tagged. I'll let you finish the story.

You can make up whatever scenario you want in business, politics, governmental agencies, the military; without truth and knowability being recognized as of utmost importance in the workplace it is only a matter of time before something goes boom, literally and/or figuratively. The problem is cultural. Millennials in particular have hit a steep downward slope in this area. The workplace must move back toward truth and knowability that is aligned with the unique culture being promoted within and by the company.

I will begin with the workplace as the place where all generations will rise up and recapture truth and knowability. This will be the first step of recapturing it for us all, throughout our culture. I believe there exists a desperate need in the U.S. to recapture truth and knowability through new philosophical and theological Millennial heroes. This will take at least another decade or two to accomplish.

As I have emphasized repeatedly, business success increasingly hinges on a Connected Age workplace environment that promotes communication, cooperation, collaboration, and co-creation (C4) among all generations. This is at the center of what many are calling "cultural transformation." In addition, the number-one driver of Millennial EPL is vocational development, career path advancement, and work/life balance.

Truth and Knowability | Value of Company Values

These top drivers for Millennial EPL are the perfect points at which culturally specific truth and knowability can be transmitted to everyone in your organization, or what is called the workplace framework.

The workplace framework refers to the cultural structure that is a part of every aspect of a business from the top office to the broom closet attendant. It is what everyone is supposed to "know" and adhere to in terms of workplace environment, company technical standards, fiduciary duties, ethics, and morals. The framework is typically established, articulated, measured, enforced and maintained by the top executives with assistance from empowered leaders and managers at lower levels and administered by human resources. To infuse the concepts of truth and knowability into the framework, my recommendation is to define the company's core value statements and include them in the framework.

These core values should be defined by the creators of the company culture (i.e. the executive team) and be included in every interview and on-boarding and reinforced regularly at every level and in every department of the organization. This process ensures that "who you are" as a company is understood by everyone. Who you are is influenced by what you value. These company "truths" are expected to be "known" and adhered to unless otherwise directed. If your company core values are not written down somewhere—it's time to do that.

It is best to limit the list to between five and seven core values. Each core value is a word or short phrase that exudes the essence of the company regarding the big topics that are influenced by your culture. This includes the people, customers, services and/or products, and ethics of the business. The objective is to define your expectation within your company regarding each core value identified. These are not dictionary definitions, rather ideas developed by leadership that are culturally relevant regarding the truth trying to be communicated and supported by each core value. And for each definition, an example or two is a big help in getting talent to understand the core value and how it can play out in the workplace.

Let's imagine "excellence" as a core value of HRbitz, a company that provides customized software tools for HR departments in large organizations. Excellence is a very broad term that can mean a lot of different things to people in different settings. The executive team for HRbitz sits down and tries to define what they mean by this core value and they realize they don't have a clue. Jim pipes up and says, "Excellence is the standard we expect every customer to think of when they load and use our programs." Susan disagrees with Jim and says, "Excellence is what we expect from our talent when they are working on any project of any size." This could go on for a while and is reflective of the subjectivity of words; what may be true for Jim is not the same for Susan.

This is not an exercise in futility but rather an eye-opening exercise for executive teams to define their core values in accordance with their own cultural practices. The word excellence refers to a measurement against a standard of some kind. The executive team is acting as the ultimate authority for establishing that standard for truth and knowability using the company's core values.

The HRbitz executives in the example above need to articulate the standard for excellence and a metric of measurement that differentiates excellence from other possibilities such as below standard, average, good, etc. This measurement establishes for them what they want to infuse in their work culture with and pass on to their talent. How will HRbitz talent understand and measure excellence? Next, they provide a real example of what excellence looks like in their culture so it can be known. Finally, the executive team presents their core value definitions to a select group of employees familiar with the company culture to solicit their comments and possible improvements. Once finalized, the defined core values are presented across the workplace framework with regular reinforcement until they become embedded in the culture of HRbitz. Moving forward, talent is routinely asked to observe and validate when excellence is being met and observe and communicate, cooperate, collaborate, and co-create (C4) with appropriate personnel when it falls short.

Establishing words that have specific meaning within the culture of your organization will allow your core values to mean something. In turn, those values will elicit responses within your organization that guide everyone forward. This model works for all generations. When new on-boarded hires show up for their first day, they will know the standard of expectation by which the core values are realized.

In addition, you are providing a vernacular that is common across all generations within your organization. Everyone can use it to avoid communication difficulties. For example, a shift supervisor on inspection may note that the wrong flooring was installed on the jobsite. The flooring

Truth and Knowability | Value of Company Values

installer argues the flooring delivery driver forgot to load the premium flooring ordered and specified in the construction plans, so the installers used the standard flooring that they found in abundant supply on the jobsite. "Once it is stained no one will notice," he said. Having something in the company clearly defined (i.e. core values) allows the shift supervisor to counsel the flooring installer that words have specific meaning, especially on construction drawings. After the counseling session, the supervisor instructs the flooring installer to carefully remove and salvage for reuse, if possible, the flooring just installed and to install the specified premium flooring once it is delivered.

As the realization that words have specific meaning filters down through the organization, requests will trickle up the chain to tie down additional words commonly used in the company that have been open to interpretation. Addressing these additional words on a case by case basis will expose any misinterpretations and contrast them to the standard definitions established in the core values.

Expanding this exercise beyond your own company might mean requesting from your vendors and subcontractors their core values. Compare them with your own and determine if, according to your values, you are in business with the right partners. For those you have concerns about, ask them to clarify their core values and share with them the experience you have had doing the same. Using Connected Age C4 opportunities you will influence companies around you and reinforce to the talent within your own company the importance of upholding the standards which create your culture and make your organization a great place to work.

Have confidence this is not only the right thing to do but something that will resonate positivity throughout the workplace. Mankind's history is replete with established and well documented ethical and moral standards based upon what philosophers have historically termed natural law. Virtually all cultures in recorded history, no matter their religious or agnostic/atheistic views, established and enforced societal laws against such things as murder, theft, and adultery. Unrestrained lawlessness within a culture is always restricted to an extreme minority. It is up to the Millennials to carry-on the demonstrated duty of all mankind and stand up against unrestrained lawlessness and condemn it in the culture and to

Unleash The Millennials and Save the World

reestablish acceptable standards of moral and ethical behavior beginning in the workplace.

The end is near. Read on for a summary of our journey and an explanation of what our future holds when the millennium change cycle (MCC) tsunami hits. I'm a glass-half-full person. Take heart and have hope. Unleash The Millennials and Save the World.

Chapter 21

Dawn of Millennial Age | Unleashed Millennials

Here we are at the end of the book entitled Unleash The Millennials and Save the World and what have we learned and where are we going? Initially we learned about the older two generations in the workplace. Who are the Boomers and why are there so few Xers in the workplace? We next explored the topic of work and discovered real generational differences exist in the workplace as to the expectation of work itself. Unleash The Millennials and Save the World.

    We learned that a lot has happened to our world and culture since the mid-1950s, including the initiation of a millennium change cycle (MCC) tsunami that will eventually culminate in millennium change within the next two generations. The MCC tsunami (accelerated by the recent pandemic) resulted from two massive cultural "Age" shifts. The first was the collapse of the Modern Philosophy and end of a 2600 year run of the Age of Western Philosophy as we know it. The philosophic void was quickly filled by the artifacts of what helped bring down Modern Philosophy and is now termed the Postmodern period of extreme skepticism and cynicism about any truth or knowability claims. The second shift was the business model paradigm as the underlying areas of economics, technology, and pedagogy transitioned from an Industrial Age business model paradigm to a completely different Connected Age business model paradigm. Unleash The Millennials and Save the World.

Unleash The Millennials and Save the World

With all that as background we finally jumped into who were the Millennials and what makes them possibly the greatest generation in human history. Millennials are no longer kids but strong, capable, technologically superior to predecessors, cooperative, creative, and innovative to just name a few attributes; and they are the key to saving the world as we know it today—bar none! And now more than ever, given our current status in the U.S., enterprises of all sectors need to immediately Unleash The Millennials and Save the World.

We examined coaching and why it is the superior learning option perfect for Millennials and all generations to infuse the principles of meaning, purpose, and calling into the workplace through an engagement, productivity, and loyalty (EPL) Coaching program that fosters creativity and innovation moving forward. Our hope is that we gain some assurance that we have a future moving forward. Unleash The Millennials and Save the World.

Once we learned why Millennials needed to be unleashed, we examined multiple key ways to do so in the workplace. These included coaching, the establishment of Next Generation Leader (NGL) initiatives, formation of Millennial dream teams, optimization of organizational leadership, institutional knowledge transfer, and succession implementation. The recommendation was to use all the key ways in order of priority. Unleash The Millennials and Save the World.

Recapturing truth and knowability in the workplace were addressed next, using company core values. This company by company establishment of local truths and knowability will, we hope, slow the bad consequence that will ensue in our postmodern culture if it is allowed to remain unchecked. Unleash The Millennials and Save the World.

It will be a decade or two before transcendent truth and knowability are reestablished within a culturally accepted philosophical/theological age of Western Philosophy or of a philosophy not yet determined. In the meantime, a lot of bad things can happen in this time of waiting. Ultimately, a new philosophy with transcendent underpinnings will either be grounded in the ultimate authority of the traditions of Western or Eastern religions or in something or someone yet to be identified. Unleash The Millennials and Save the World.

And finally, we arrive at this question: "What will the dawn of the Millennial Age look like?" What we know now is there is a strong push within the business sector to transform culture. Now that we know why this transformation from the Industrial Age business model paradigm to a Connected Age paradigm is necessary, perhaps we'll see a little giddy-up by those slow to get on-board before the MCC tsunami arrives in 2025 or sooner. When the Millennials assume seventy-five percent of the workforce positions by 2025, they will in essence be in charge of everything! And then, as if overnight, everything will change. What do I mean by everything?

Consider just these three changes and the "everything" impact any one of them would have: 1. an entirely new digital global currency; 2. elimination of all international indebtedness; 3. establishment of true global free-trade unity. This is not a far stretch and even more likely in the wake of the global pandemic. There is no longer a standard, such as gold, for establishing currency values around the world. Connected Age thinkers already realize that few countries, if any, are in positions to ever repay their current debt in the next fifty to 1000 years or more unless we suffer global hyper-inflation. In order to prevent that and the ensuing default and global currency collapse they will likely just flip a switch and convert all private and corporate currency held in "identifiable and verifiable" banking, savings, investment, stock, etc. digital accounts and similar type digital records of individual and corporate indebtedness to a single global digital currency asset or debit. And at the rate the Federal Reserve in the U.S. is buying Federal, state, and municipal debt and corporate bonds due to the pandemic induced economic shutdown they will own all outstanding debt in the U.S. by September 2020. If that materializes, a switch to digital currency will be pretty straight forward.

That's just the first, the next two are pretty simple to do as well, using unempathetic AI technologies and systems. More difficult issues that we will encounter that have yet to be resolved include weaponized AI, global weather changes, natural disasters, cyber theft, cyber security, human-made environmental disasters, large scale involuntary migrations of people, biodiversity or ecosystem collapse, loss of clean water, antimicrobial resistance, internal civil wars or regional wars, nuclear and biological weapons proliferation, the continuing devaluation of individual life and freedom, and the list could go on for days.

Speaking of AI, by 2025 will we be more addicted to AI than we are to our current mobile devices or will we be off the grid living a pioneer type

Unleash The Millennials and Save the World

life in Idaho, Kansas, or Alaska. I just know AI is coming fast and furious into the workplace and will slam the door on the Industrial Age forever. One of my book editors requested I remove some of my examples of already available radicalized AI workplace implementations that stretched a gambit of everyday situations. The editor noted my examples made them stop reading, stopped them cold, had them shuttering of the possibilities. It wasn't that the examples were graphic, rather as the mind considers the implications of AI technologies being rolled out into the marketplace today you cannot help but stop and feel the gravity of what the Millennials will be facing. The decisions they will have to make. Who they will have to stand against to resist? This is not for the faint of heart but requires a generation of superheroes; each individually prepared in an area of expertise and empowered to act in unison with their team. The day of reckoning Boomers have been dreaming of since first being trained to hide under a desk in the case of nuclear attack is upon us. But we can avoid an ugly outcome of what is possible as we did back then, Unleash The Millennials and Save the World!

Did you know the iPhone was just introduced in 2007? Think about that; our first taste of mobile touch screen and app ready devices was a mere thirteen years ago. And now that touch screen technology is global with 5G coming on-line the Internet of Things is here. If you have bad dreams at night, don't look-up what this implies in regard to personal privacy when you have done nothing wrong to another; other than what you think, believe, who you associate with, or do not associate with.

Beyond comprehension are the disrupters AI is bringing into the workplace that will compete against existing human talent. While AI prototypes may not yet be as efficient as humans, they can be programmed to work 24/7 with learning modules that improve efficiency with each iteration of a cycle. Unleash The Millennials and Save the World quickly, or the human talent demand as we know it today will no longer exist. I recently heard of a local company that started an app for a lawn service on the Uber model (i.e. background checked talent, insured, etc.). With a few clicks you get a price, they show up same day, do the job, and your credit card is charged when they finish. How long before a drone mower is going to unload from a driverless truck? Mom and pop paper flyer in the door lawn businesses will be a thing of the past.

Dawn of Millennial Age | Unleashed Millennials

Literally every field is bursting at the seams with innovations ready to come on-line and fully developed by 2025. 3-D printing of everything including full scale buildings, Google glasses that will act like a heads-up display of everything around you, smart devices everywhere, laptop supercomputers, self-driving cars, biometrics and genetic security for everything, and these just scratch the surface.

Millennials in 2025 will inherit all the problems Boomers started and refused to address and finish. These problems exist in every corner of the world and with every sector of our human social construct; we've piled a lot of social and cultural garbage in the closets of the world that the Millennials and Gen-Z will have to clean up. The process of bringing us back from the ledge in so many areas will contribute to the rapidity of the millennium change I've alluded to several times in the book. This change will likely happen within the next one to two generations and coincide with the establishment of a new philosophy with transcendent foundational support. What might this millennium change look like?

Perhaps they will start with openly revealing the U.S. and others have already developed antigravity hyper-sonic aircraft (i.e. flying saucers). Perhaps they will also begin global distribution of 21st century free energy systems initially developed by Nikola Tesla in 1901 (U.S. Patent 685,957 – Apparatus for The Utilization of Radiant Energy). Both of these disrupters would dramatically impact fossil fuels that currently dominate and control all global economic markets and economies. These announcements would likely happen coincidentally with the establishment of an entirely new digital global currency mentioned earlier. NOTE: The global digital currency is key to global sustainability. Did someone just predict levitation, free energy, sustainability, elimination of fossil fuel emissions, digital global currency, and no debt? I'm not crazy, just sane enough to realize Boomers will not be here to stop it.

For Boomers, we never believed we'd see a Dick Tracy wristwatch yet I'm wearing one on my wrist today. The question is, "Will my grandchildren be driving my wife and I around in a Fred and Wilma Flint mobile in thirty years (I'll only be ninety-one) or will they be taking us riding in a George and Jane Jetson self-flying saucer?" I'd much prefer the self-flying saucer sported about by George and Jane. One thing I know, and know for sure, the Millennials will be in charge soon, whether you

Unleash The Millennials and Save the World

like it or not. Now rather than later is the time to Unleash The Millennials and Save the World.

Let them recapture truth and knowability in the workplace. Let them figure out how to transform your company into a Connected Age business model before the MCC tsunami hits in 2025. Let them figure out how to establish a philosophy that reestablishes transcendent truth and knowability to a single authority outside of ourselves. Let them with Gen-Z figure out what our millennium change will look like. Either good or catastrophic, they, our children, and our grandchildren will be the ones who will have to deal with the consequences of their decisions.

Our job now as Boomers and older Xers is to infuse as quickly as possible those things we know and believe will help them make the right choices moving forward. Our best access to Millennials is in the workplace. And what a win-win!! We provide Millennials the opportunity to discover life meaning, individual purpose, and affirm vocational calling while enhancing their EPL for creativity and innovation to solve not just our corporate issues, but local, regional, national, and global issues of our day and tomorrow. "UNLEASH THE MILLENNIALS – AND SAVE THE WORLD!"

As you do, I'll be working alongside you in earnest through Engineering Leadership Design Company, LLC, ZIMMERMAN Coaching Group, and Kitesurfers Academy to prepare workplaces across the U.S. for the impending MCC tsunami. If after reading this book you want to communicate, cooperate, collaborate, or co-create something together connect with me through UnleashTheMillennials.com. I'd love the opportunity to begin a conversation. Unleash The Millennials and Save the World.

END NOTES

Chapter 1

1. Economy, Peter, "The (Millennial) Workplace of the Future Is Almost Here -- These 3 Things Are About to Change Big Time," Inc. on-line, Jan. 15, 2019, last accessed Apr. 26, 2019, https://www.inc.com/peter-economy/the-millennial-workplace-of-future-is-almost-here-these-3-things-are-about-to-change-big-time.html
2. Ibid
3. Suster, Mark, "Mark Cuban on Why You Need to Study Artificial Intelligence or You'll be a Dinosaur in 3 Years," Both Sides, Feb 7, 2017, last accessed Aug. 20, 2019, https://bothsidesofthetable.com/mark-cuban-on-why-you-need-to-study-artificial-intelligence-or-youll-be-a-dinosaur-in-3-years-db3447bea1b4
4. Clifford, Catherine, "Mark Cuban on dangers of A.I.: If you don't think Terminator is coming, 'you're crazy,'" CNBC, 25 July 2018, https://www.cnbc.com/ 2018/07/25/mark-cuban-dangers-of-ai-terminator-is-coming.html
5. Ibid.
6. Economy, Peter, "The (Millennial) Workplace of the Future Is Almost Here -- These 3 Things Are About to Change Big Time," Inc. on-line, Jan. 15, 2019, last accessed Apr. 26, 2019, https://www.inc.com/peter-economy/the-millennial-workplace-of-future-is-almost-here-these-3-things-are-about-to-change-big-time.html
7. Ibid

Chapter 2

8. Martin Anderson, "The Reagan Boom - Greatest Ever," The New York Times, Jan. 17, 1990, last accessed April 25, 2019, https://www.nytimes.com/1990/01/17/ opinion/the-reagan-boom-greatest-ever.html.

Chapter 6

9. Ray Williams, "How Millennials Are Transforming Careers and the Workplace," Psychology Today, September 16, 2013, accessed October 3, 2014, https://www.psychologytoday.com/ blog/wired-success/201309/how-millennials-are-transforming-careers-and-the-workplace.
10. Scott, Robert E., "Manufacturing Job Loss – Trade, Not Productivity, Is the Culprit," Economic Policy Institute, August 11, 2015, last accessed February 27, 2019, https://www.epi.org/publication/manufacturing-job-loss-trade-not-productivity-is-the-culprit.
11. James A. Dewar, "The Information Age and The Printing Press: Looking Backward to See Ahead," Rand Corporation, accessed October 1, 2014, http://www.rand.org/pubs/papers/P8014/index2.html#fn0.
12. Ibid
13. Evan Rosen, "Every Worker is a Knowledge Worker," Bloomberg Business Week, January 11, 2011, accessed October 2, 2014, http://www.businessweek.com/ managing/content/jan2011/ca20110110_985915.htm.

[14] David Russell Schilling, "Knowledge Doubling Every 12 Months, Soon to be Every 12 Hours," Industry Tap, April 19, 2013, accessed October 1, 2014, http://www.industrytap.com/knowledge-doubling-every-12-months-soon-to-be-every-12-hours/3950.
[15] Ibid.
[16] Alex Durand, "Why Millennials Need To Fight For Work-Life Integration," EliteDaily.com, November 30, 2014, accessed February 16, 2015, http://elitedaily.com/life/millennials-work-life-integration/854899/.
[17] Laura Vanderkam, "How Many Hours Should You Be Working," Fortune, June 6, 2011, accessed October 13, 2014, http://fortune.com/2011/06/06/how-many-hours-should-you-be-working/.

Chapter 10

[18] Jane Bluestein, "Industrial Age Vs. Information Age," Janebluestein.com, accessed October 1, 2014, http://janebluestein.com/2012/industrial-age-vs-information-age/.
[19] Anne Zelenka, "From The Information Age To The Connected Age," GIGAOM, October 6, 2007, accessed October 1, 2014, https://gigaom.com/2007/10/06/from-the-information-age-to-the-connected-age/.
[20] Ibid.
[21] Virginia Heffernan, "Education Needs a Digital-Age Upgrade," New York Times, August 7, 2011, accessed October 2, 2014, http://opinionator.blogs.nytimes.com/2011/08/07/education-needs-a-digital-age-upgrade/?_php=true&_type=blogs&_r=0.
[22] Gloria Larson, The Prepared U Project, An In-Depth Look at Millennial Preparedness for Today's WorkForce (Boston, MA: Bentley University, 2014), eBook, accessed October 1, 2014, https://www.bentley.edu/files/prepared/ 1.29.2013_BentleyU_Whitepaper_Shareable.pdf.
[23] Bentley University, "The Prepared U Project, An Infographic Storybook on Millennials in the Workplace," accessed October 1, 2014, http://www.slideshare.net/BentleyU/prepared-u-project-Millennials-in-the-workplace.
[24] Ibid.

Chapter 11

[25] U. S. Chamber of Commerce Foundation, "The Millennial Generation Research Review," USChamberfoundation.org, accessed November 5, 2014, http://www.uschamberfoundation.org/ millennial-generation-research-review.
[26] O'Reilly, Brian, "Meet The Future It's Your Kids the Millennial Generation Has Grown Up With Prosperity, the Internet, Divorce, and Columbine. They Already Know They Don't Want to Live or Work the Way We Do," Fortune, July 24, 2000, accessed March 12, 2014, http://archive.fortune.com/magazines/fortune/fortune_archive/2000/07/24/284656/index.htm.
[27] Ibid.
[28] Ibid.
[29] Ibid.
[30] Ibid.
[31] Ibid.
[32] Neil Howe and Bill Strauss, Millennials Rising: The Next Great Generation (New York: Vintage Books, 2000).
[33] Ibid. 4
[34] Worldcat Search Results on Millennial Generation, accessed March 13, 2015, http://www.worldcat.org/search?q=millennial+generation&fq=dt%3Aart&dblist=638&fc=yr:_25&qt=show_more_yr%3A&cookie.
[35] Pew Research Center, How Young People View Their Lives, Futures and Politics, A Portrait of "Generation Next, 1st ed. (Washington: The Pew Research Center, 2007), eBook, accessed March 13, 2015, http://www.people-press.org/files/legacy-pdf/300.pdf.
[36] Pew Research Center, Millennials, Confident. Connected. Open to Change, 1st ed. (Washington: The Pew Research Center, 2010), eBook, accessed October 2, 2014,

End Notes

http://www.pewsocialtrends.org/files/ 2010/10/millennials-confident-connected-open-to-change.pdf.

[37] Tim Elmore, Generation iY Our Last Chance to Save Their Future (Atlanta, GA: Post Gardner, 2010), 19–28.

[38] Tim Elmore, Artificial Maturity Helping Kids Meet The Challenge of Becoming Authentic Adults (San Francisco, CA: Jossey-Bass, 2012), 90.

[39] Jeanne Meister and Karie Willyerd, "Mentoring Millennials," Harvard Business Review, May 2010, accessed October 1, 2014, http://hbr.org/2010/05/mentoring-Millennials/.

[40] Jessica Brack, Unlocking the Potential of On-Demand Learning in the Workplace (Chapel Hill, NC: UNC Kenan-Flagler Business School, 2010), 1, accessed March 7, 2015, http://www.kenan-flagler.unc.edu/ executive-development/custom-programs/~/media/DF1C11C056874DDA8097271A1ED48662.ashx.

[41] Steinmetz, Krystal. "Employers Don't Think Much of Millennials' Work Ethic." MoneyTalksNews, May 26, 2014, Accessed September 28, 2014.
http://www.moneytalksnews.com/2014/05/26/employers-dont-think-much-of-Millennials-work-ethic/.

[42] Hartman, Mitchell. "Millennials at Work: Young and Callow, Like Their Parents." The New York Times, March 24, 2014. Accessed September 28, 2014. http://www.nytimes.com/2014/03/25/your-money/Millennials-at-work-young-and-callow-like-their-parents.html?_r=0.

[43] Graves, Jada. "Millennial Workers: Entitled, Needy, Self-Centered?" U.S. News & World Report, June 27, 2012. Accessed September 28, 2014.
http://money.usnews.com/money/careers/articles/2012/06/27/Millennial-workers-entitled-needy-self-centered.

[44] Greg Willard, "New Data Tells Some Surprising Truths about Millennials," January 7, 2015, accessed February 28, 2015, http://www.tlnt.com/2015/01/07/new-data-tells-some-surprising-truths-about-millennials/.

[45] Michael Marciniak, "The Truth About Millennials." AdvisorsAhead, December 19, 2014, accessed February 28, 2015, http://www.advisorsahead.com/the-truth-about-millennials/.

[46] Marion White, Rethinking Generation Gaps in the Workplace: Focus on Shared Values, (Chapel Hill, NC: UNC Kenan-Flagler Business School, 2011), 5, accessed March 7, 2015, http://www.kenan-flagler.unc.edu/executive-development/about/~/media/C8FC09AEF03743BE91112418FEE286D0.ashx., 8.

[47] PR Newswire, "Employers need to rely on workforce analytics to help employees thrive." February 19, 2015, accessed February 28, 2015, http://www.multivu.com/players/English/7428151-ibm-millennials-workplace-myths/.

[48] Ibid.

[49] Carolyn Heller Baird, Myths, Exaggerations And Uncomfortable Truths, The Real Story Behind Millennials In The Workplace (Somers, NY: IBM Corporation, 2015), 1, accessed February 28, 2015, http://public.dhe.ibm.com/common/ssi/ecm/gb/en/gbl03032usen/GBL03032USEN.PDF.

[50] Baird, Myths, Exaggerations And Uncomfortable Truths, The Real Story Behind Millennials In The Workplace, 10–13.

[51] Whitney Ricketts, "Inaugural Creative Jobs Report Reveals New American Dream," CreativeLive.com, March 27, 2014, accessed March 7, 2015, http://blog.creativelive.com/creative-jobs-report/.

[52] Joseph Coombs, "Generational Change in the Workplace, Workplace Visions, Society of Human Resource Management, no. 1 (2014), accessed November 11, 2014, https://www.shrm.org/Research/FutureWorkplaceTrends/Documents/14-0081%20Workplace%20Visions%20Issue_1_ 2014_viewonlyFNL.pdf.

[53] Ibid.

[54] Ross Pomeroy and William Handke, "The Most Entitled Generation Isn´t Millennials. It´s Baby Boomers." January 9, 2015, accessed March 7, 2015, http://www.realclearpolitics.com/articles/2015/01/09/the_most_entitled_generation_isnt_millennials_its_baby_boomers_125184.html.

[55] Ibid.

[56] B. J. Kito, "The Shocking Truth About Millennials," AdWeek, June 27, 2014, accessed February 28, 2015, http://www.adweek.com/prnewser/the-shocking-truth-about-millennials/95888.

[57] Ibid.

58 Clifton, Jim, "How Millennials Want to Work and Live – The Six Big Changes Leaders Have to Make" Gallup.com, last Accessed August 19, 2019, https://www.gallup.com/workplace/238073/millennials-work-live.aspx

59 Ibid

Chapter 12

60 John Harter, Employee Engagement of the Rise in the U.S., Gallup, August, 26, 2018, last accessed March 19, 2019, https://news.gallup.com/poll/241649/employee-engagement-rise.aspx.

61 Ibid

62 Sharon Ting and Peter Scisco, ed., "Introduction," in The Center for Christian Leadership Handbook of Coaching (San Francisco, CA: Jossey-Bass, 2006), 10–11.

63 Tim Theeboom, Bianca Beersma, and Annelies E.M. van Vianen, "Does Coaching Work? A Meta-Analysis on the Effects of Coaching on Individual Level Outcomes in an Organizational Context," The Journal of Positive Psychology 9, no.1 (2013): 1-18, accessed October 28, 2015, http://www.tandfonline.com.ezproxy.dts.edu/doi/pdf/10.1080/17439760.2013.837499.

64 Berkovitz, Lisa. "Why Coaching Is The Second Fastest Growing Industry in The World." Up Market Magazine. April 10, 2012. Accessed October 1, 2014. http://upmarketzine.com/2012/04/10/why-coaching-is-the-second-fastest-growing-industry-in-the-world/

65 Peer Resources, "Coach Training Programs and Schools," Peer Resources, Last updated Jul. 25, 2018, accessed Mar. 16, 2019, https://www.peer.ca/coachingschoolsintro.html.

66 Peer Resources, "Coach Training Programs and Schools."

67 Ibid.

68 Leadership Coaching Services, Individual, Team And Skills Development (Greensboro, NC: Center for Creative Leadership (CCL), 2015), accessed October 31, 2015, http://www.ccl.org/Leadership/pdf/coaching/LeadershipCoaching.pdf.

69 Dave Buck, Play to Win Method Playbook (Hopatcong, NJ: Self-Published Coachville, 2014), 20.

70 Sullivan, Brian. "How to Coach the Millennials on Your Sales Team." Sandler.com, November 3, 2014. Accessed November 24, 2014. http://www.sandler.com/blog/how-to-coach-millennials-sales-team/.

71 Karen Albritton, The Truth About Millennial Workers, 1st ed. (Raleigh, NC: capstrat, 2011), eBook, accessed October 1, 2014, https://www.capstrat.com/elements/downloads/files/millennials-work.pdf.

72 Jessica Brack, Unlocking the Potential of On-Demand Learning in the Workplace , 9.

73 White, Rethinking Generation Gaps in the Workplace, 8.

74 Abby Ellin, "The Beat (Up) Generation," Psychology Today, March 22, 2014, accessed March 16, 2015, http://www.psychologytoday.com/articles/201402/the-beat-generation.

75 SAP. Workforce 2020, The Looming Talent Crisis, SuccessFactors.com, 2014. Accessed October 1, 2014. http://www.successfactors.com/en_us/download.html?a=/content/dam/successfactors/en_us/resources/white-papers/sap-workforce2020-executive-summary.pdf.

76 Meister and Willyerd, "Mentoring Millennials."

77 Ibid.

78 Deloitte, Big Demands and High Expectations, The Deloitte Millennial Survey (New York: Deloitte Touche Tohmatsu Limited, January 2014), accessed October 1, 2014, https://www2.deloitte.com/content/dam/Deloitte/global/Documents/About-Deloitte/gx-dttl-2014-millennial-survey-report.pdf.

79 Ibid.

Chapter 13

80 John Harter, Employee Engagement of the Rise in the U.S., Gallup, August 26, 2018, last accessed March 19, 2019, https://news.gallup.com/poll/241649/employee-engagement-rise.aspx.

81 Ibid.

82 Ibid.

83 Clay Robinson, The Real Cost of Employee Disengagement, February 14, 2018, shiftboard, last accessed March 29, 2018, https://www.shiftboard.com/blog/real-cost-employee-disengagement/

End Notes

[84] Gallup, How Millennials Want to Work and Live, 2016, Gallup, Inc., last accessed March 29, 2019, https://www.gallup.com/workplace/238073/millennials-work-live.aspx.

[85] Kruse, Kevin. "What is Employee Engagement." *Forbes*, June 6 2012, Accessed October 3, 2014. http://www.forbes.com/sites/kevinkruse/2012/06/220empoyee-engagement-what-and-why

[86] David Macleod, "What is Employee Engagement?" Engage for Success, accessed October 1, 2014, http://www.engageforsuccess.org/about/what-is-employee-engagement/.

[87] Ibid.

[88] Omar Ramzy, Randa El Bedawy, Aya Maher, Dysfunctional Behavior at the Workplace and Its Impact on Employees' Job Performance, International Journal of Business Administration, Vol. 9, No. 4, 2018, July 30, 2018, last accessed Apr. 7, 2019, www.sciedupress.com/journal/index.php/ijba/article/download/13944/8599.

[89] Ibid, 229

[90] Ibid, 230

[91] Ibid 230

[92] David MacLeod and Nita Clarke, Engaging for Success: Enhancing Performance Through Employee Engagement, 1st ed. (Norwich: The National Archives UK, 2008), eBook, accessed March 18, 2015, http://www.engageforsuccess.org/wp-content/uploads/2012/09/file52215.pdf.

[93] Ibid

[94] MacLeod and Clarke, Engaging for Success: Enhancing Performance Through Employee Engagement.

[95] Dennis Finn and Anne Donova, PwC's NextGen: A GlobalGgenerational Study, Evolving Talent Strategy to Match to New Workforce Reality (New York: PwC, 2013), accessed March 7, 2015, http://www.pwc.com/us/en/people-management/publications/nextgen-global-generational-study.jhtml.

[96] Baton Rouge Business Report, "Getting Engaged," BusinessReport.com, January 21, 2014, accessed March 7, 2015, http://www.businessreport.com/article/getting-engaged-2.

[97] Derrick Feldmann, The Millennial Impact Report 2013, (West Palm Beach, FL: Forte Interactive, Inc., 2013), 9, accessed March 7, 2014, http://cdn.trustedpartner.com/docs/library/AchieveMCON2013/ Research%20Report/Millennial%20Impact%20Research.pdf.

[98] Crowley, Mark C. "How SAS Became The World's Best Place To Work." FastCompany.com. January 22, 2013. Accessed October 4, 2014. http://www.fastcompany.com/3004953/how-sas-became-worlds-best-place-work.

[99] Ibid.

[100] Ibid.

[101] Ibid.

[102] Susan Sorenson and Keri Garman, "There's A Generation Gap In Your Workplace," Gallup Business Journal, August 6, 2013, accessed August 27, 2014, http://businessjournal.gallup.com/content/163466/generation-gap-workplace.aspx.

[103] https://www.gallup.com/workplace/238073/millennials-work-live.aspx, last accessed April 30, 2020

[104] Ibid

[105] Gallup, How Millennials Want to Work and Live, 2016, Gallup, Inc., last accessed March 29, 2019, https://www.gallup.com/workplace/238073/millennials-work-live.aspx.

[106] Victor Lipman, "7 Management Practices That Can Improve Employee Productivity," Forbes, June 17, 2013, accessed October 1, 2014, http://www.forbes.com/sites/victorlipman/2013/06/17/7-management-practices-that-can-improve-employee-productivity/print/.

[107] Ibid.

[108] Chad Halvorson, "The Complete Guide To Improving Employee Productivity," WhenIWork.com, October 1, 2013, accessed October 1, 2014, http://wheniwork.com/blog/the-complete-guide-to-improving-employee-productivity/.

[109] Feldman, Mark. "10 Unusual Ways to Improve Employee Productivity." SwitchandShift.com, April 23, 2014. Accessed October 1, 2014. http://switchandshift.com/10-unusual-ways-to-improve-employee-productivity.

[110] Nicole Fallon, "4 Unconventional Ways to Increase Employee Productivity," Business News Daily, December 15, 2013, accessed October 14, 2014, http://www.businessnewsdaily.com/5622-policies-improve-productivity-morale.html.

[111] Jenny Dearborn, "Eight Tactics to Increase Millienial Productivity in The Workplace," Forbes, September 20, 2013, accessed October 1, 2014,

http://www.forbes.com/sites/sap/2013/09/20/eight-tactics-to-increase-Millennial-productivity-in-the-workplace/print/.

[112] Hamilton, Kathryn. "On-Site Productivity, Engagement and Comfort Drive Next Generation of Millennial-Based Office Designs." NAIOP. August 19, 2014. Accessed October 1, 2014. http://www.naiop.org/en/About-NAIOP/News/NAIOP-News/2014/On-site-Productivity-Engagement-and-Comfort-Drive-Next-Generation.aspx?p=1.

[113] Ibid.

[114] Demetrios Gianniris, The Millennial Arrival And The Evolution Of The Modern Workplace, Forbes, January 25, 2018, last accessed March 15, 2019, https://www.forbes.com/sites/forbestechcouncil/2018/01/25/the-millennial-arrival-and-the-evolution-of-the-modern-workplace/#40a480865a73.

[115] Ibid

[116] Ibid

[117] Millennial Branding Company, "The Loyal Millennial," Millennial Branding Company, accessed October 1, 2014, http://www.slideshare.net/JLL/theloyalmillenniumthenextgenerationof-employees.

[118] Ibid.

[119] Beyond.com, "The Great Divide, Workplace Perceptions That Millennials Need to Rise Above."

[120] Instructure.com, last accessed April 30, 2020, https://www.getbridge.com/news/press-releases/millennials-are-most-likely-stay-loyal-jobs-development-opportunities

[121] Phaneuf, Wendy. "Employee Loyalty Doesn't Equal Longevity." Leading For Loyalty. Accessed October 1, 2014. http://www.leadingforloyalty.com/employee_loyalty.html.

[122] Kyle LaMalfa, "The Top 11 Ways to Increase Your Employee Loyalty," Allegiance, accessed October 1, 2014, http://www.customerservicegroup.com/pdf/allegianceincreaseloyalty.pdf.

[123] Crowley, "How SAS Became The World's Best Place To Work."

[124] Ibid.

[125] Ibid.

[126] Ibid.

[127] Josh Tolan, "Don't Ignore the Cultural Perks Millennials Crave on the Job," Enterpreneur.Com, May 27, 2014, accessed October 1, 2014, http://www.entrepreneur.com/article/234190.

[128] Towers Watson. 2014 Global M&A Retention Survey, How Companies Use Agreements to Keep Top Talent. TowersWatson.com, 2014. Accessed October 24, 2014. http://www.towerswatson.com/en-US/Insights/IC-Types/Survey-Research-Results/2014/10/2014-global-ma-retention-survey-report.

[129] BAYT, "The Drivers of Employee Loyalty in Today's Workplace," BAYT.com, 2008, accessed October 1, 2014, http://www.bayt.com/en/career-article-2501/.

[130] Anne Claire Broughton, Embracing Open-Book Management to Fuel Employee Engagement and Corporate Sustainability (Chapel Hill, NC: UNC Kenan-Flagler Business School, 2012), 7, eBook, accessed October 1, 2014, http://www.kenan-flagler.unc.edu/executive-development/custom-programs/~/media/C910D7FE40984DAF8DFD90A37335E452.ashx.

[131] Jessica Brack, Unlocking the Potential of On-Demand Learning in the Workplace, 12.

[132] Crowley, "How SAS Became The World's Best Place To Work."

www.ingramcontent.com/pod-product-compliance
Lightning Source LLC
Chambersburg PA
CBHW072028230526
45466CB00020B/1055